# Big Girls Don't Cry

## IVANA IVANCAKOVA

I_AM SELF-PUBLISHING

@iamselfpub
www.iamselfpublishing.com

Dedicated to my parents, Anna and Jan, my brother, Jan, my little princess, and the love of my life…

# Contents

# Prologue

*The Green Mile.* I don't even know why I was watching the movie. I prefer more romantic films or chick flicks – ones where you know there will be a happy ever after ending. *The Green Mile* has too many male characters and too much negative energy for my taste. Most of it is set in prison, which is a little bit depressing. Well, very depressing, actually.

I was sitting on the sofa, all wrapped up in a blanket, eating a blueberry muffin and watching a bald man domesticate a mouse. He was laughing at it in a crazy way. He loved that mouse just like a child, and was happy to snuggle up to it. Urgh! It made me shiver when he put his face right next to the mouse, and I wondered what could cause this kind of madness and desperation.

I was so tired, I started yawning, but watched the movie until the end, even though it left me feeling very negative, as the story included a sad, innocent prisoner, a bad, insecure prison officer, and a crazy killer of little girls.

"Come on, it's only a story you know," my flatmate, Alisha, said when I kept going on about it the next day. I shook my head and left the house, unable to get the wretched image out of my head. I had no idea that I'd also be sitting in a prison cell in just a few weeks' time, so unhappy that I'd be willing to give away half of my wardrobe for a little mouse like that.

# 1

## Food

"Why don't you eat?"

"I do."

"No, you don't."

"I eat as much as I need to; I never stuff myself."

"You look to me like you don't eat enough."

"I know that better than you," I replied. I didn't want to be rude, just confident.

"Your relationship with food is simply anorexic."

"Whatever."

"Why are you doing this to yourself?"

"What do you mean?"

"Why are you starving yourself? Just because you are a model?"

"No, it's not like that at all."

"Why then?"

"I am not starving myself. I don't like a full belly. I feel better when I eat healthy and light."

"But you are extremely skinny."

"I was always like this; I was born early."

"Look after yourself, Ivana."

His words were kind but firm. I don't know if the prison psychologist was nice to all the women in there, but every time I left his office, I felt a tiny bit better. He was a human I could talk to in that hell. He always spoke in English to me, which was more than you could say about some of the

French people that worked in the prison, who liked to make life difficult for me. He was the only person I could talk to and cry in front of if I wanted to. Sometimes, I didn't want to see anyone at all. When you are in prison, there are times when you don't want to do anything, nothing at all. The longer you are there, the worse it gets, especially if you are innocent.

Maybe he was right when he mentioned anorexia.

Fashion was always my world, but I was the ugly duckling for most of my childhood and teenage years. I just sat in the corner, reading books, dreaming about the big world out there.

My father was a very strict, rigorous and conservative person, who was quite OK with the fact that I had no confidence at all and lived my life mostly through books.

The clubs, where my girlfriends partied away during their teenage years, didn't interest me. Even if I had wanted to go, I knew that my father would not let me, so I just dreamed about my own future life – a life full of bling, clothes, shoes, runways and the flash of cameras. Sometimes, I would enter casting competitions, but I really lacked confidence back then. For me, modelling was just a dream.

I grew up in the kind of small village where everybody seemed to know each other's business, but many people didn't even know me because I spent most of my time with my books and magazines. I was one of those nice, polite, shy girls who never talked very much.

Nobody ever knew that in my own little world, I was walking down the catwalk, wearing clothes by the world's most famous designers. Maybe that's why I came to England when I was 18. I had changed a lot by then. It was a fresh start. I didn't have a past.

I wanted to prove to myself, and to the whole world, that I was worth it; that I was beautiful. So I didn't eat much. If I did eat a little bit more, I didn't feel well. This meant I ended up in hospital a few times after passing out because I was exhausted and hungry.

I never listened to anybody. I only ate once a day, mostly chocolate or blueberry muffins and coffee, sometimes a jacket potato with salad.

I really don't know why, I had some kind of block in my head. I am much better now, eat much more food and take more exercise.

# 2

# Southampton

I came to England on 21<sup>st</sup> November 2002, just before my 18<sup>th</sup> birthday, which was in December. I was an au pair in Southampton for a lovely family with three kids.

The youngest was only eight months old, and the oldest was six. I didn't stop working for a minute, but really enjoyed it. I found it exciting to be in a new environment with a different mentality, speaking a different language – everything was different. I grew in confidence, met some lovely people, and my English really improved.

After a year, when I was able to speak English better, I got a weekend job at the pub, as I needed to be around grown-ups, not just children! I made good friends with the regulars and was happy with my new life. Time went by so fast that I didn't even think of my parents back home, who were waiting for me to return. They did not want to let me go. They didn't understand how important and exciting it was for me to taste these new experiences. All they wanted was for me to return back home to live a normal, simple life in their village. In their eyes, "normal" meant having a husband, kids and a job not far from the village, so that you didn't have to spend a lot of money on travel. We were worlds apart.

But I loved England. There was a lot going on there and I enjoyed everything about it, even the noise. I was happy. I will never forget the first time I went into an English shoe shop. I could barely contain myself, as the styles and colours were nothing like the ones the Slovakian girls would wear back home. The range was so exciting.

"What happened to you?" my father asked angrily, when I finally came home to visit. "Did you forget who you are? Did you forget Slovakia?"

I just shook my head. "I didn't forget, Daddy, I am just living my life the way that I want to."

"What do you mean, the way you want to? Girls your age are settling down, getting married, having families, not travelling around the world."

"I don't want a family just yet!"

"Don't tell me that!"

"It's my life, Daddy, you have to understand that I don't want to get married to just anybody. I want to give my kids a real future, more opportunities than I had myself. I want to travel and live my own way. I am meeting lots of interesting people. I can be successful in England."

There was no point in arguing. He didn't understand that I couldn't see myself living my life in a small village in east Slovakia, and seemed insulted by my desire to improve my life. I was no longer the timid girl he had known when I was growing up, and he was surprised that I was no longer scared about defending my opinions. By the time I flew back to England, I felt like my family didn't understand me anymore.

\* \* \*

Back in the UK, I didn't forget my dreams about fashion. My bedroom was full of magazines and I would spend hours going through all of them to discover the latest trends. Whenever I met someone in the pub who was a little closer to the fashion industry, I would ask them lots of questions. I was in my own little world, thinking and planning ahead.

Southampton is not far from London, the city of fashion where my dreams would come true. So I knew I was close. I wanted to be one of those people whose face appears in magazines and enjoys free entry to VIP clubs, where the doors for "normal people" are closed. I wanted all of that, but I didn't want to just dream anymore. I needed to do something about it and move on.

So, after two years, when my contract was up, I left my au pair job but stayed working long hours at the pub six days a week. I got promoted to head waitress and worked mostly with students. We had good times and they encouraged me to try a course myself. Soon, every Wednesday, I was going to college do a make-up diploma. This meant most of my money at this time went on make-up, such as foundations, eye shadows, lipsticks and brushes, and I spent a lot of time working on my portfolio – using all the models I could from the pub, of course, doing before and after photos. Anybody for a makeover, ladies?

It was hard work but I loved it. I didn't have any spare time, but I knew it was what I wanted to do. My move to London would come soon, I just knew it.

I needed to move on from the pub, as I was finishing college, and could finally set out to achieve my ambitions. I was also getting fed up with pub life and, if I'm honest, was a little heartbroken too. I was dreaming about chips and beer. It was now or never.

# 3

## *London at Last*

London was the best place to start a new chapter in my life. I moved to the capital with my best friend, Alisha, who was the daughter of the pub landlord. They had become my other family, really.

I got a job as a make-up artist quite quickly, at one of the smaller modelling agencies that are on the corner of every street in London. I soon learnt that London is full of girls from all over the world, who come here to be a model and are so full of their dreams, they become prey for agencies and their fake promises.

Many of them have no idea what modelling is all about. It is not just the way you look, but who you know! You need to be different and have your own style. Many of those girls will come to London, pay crazy money for a portfolio, and never get a single modelling job. Those small agencies have no idea about fashion. They are keen to sign the girls up and talk to them about their future life, famous boyfriends etc., but for 90 per cent of these girls, it will be their first and last photo shoot.

When I became a booker in an agency, I picked a few girls that I could possibly see on a catwalk in the future and tried my best to get them jobs whenever I saw anything that might be suitable for them. These were not great jobs, but small shoots and castings for small designers.

The owner of the agency I joined was from the Middle East and had no idea about fashion. All he wanted was to make money from these poor girls, which I hated. I just couldn't stand it.

Every day it was getting worse and worse for me. I was meeting real people that were serious about fashion, who I could learn from, but in the agency, it was completely different. I was surrounded by people who had no idea about Karl Lagerfeld or Marc Jacobs.

"Just leave, you can do it without them," Alisha told me many times in the evening, while we watched *Friends*, drank coffee and ate blueberry muffins.

"I will, I promise I'll leave soon," I said, while thinking how I could fix the mess I was in.

"I think you should start to get modelling jobs for yourself, not for others," she suggested. "I am sure you can do it."

"You think so?"

"I know it."

We giggled and laughed. She was just like my sister, and she wasn't wrong. The first modelling job wasn't that far away.

# 4

# *London Fashion Week*

Si Marshall changed my life. He is an English fashion designer, who helped me to get into the real world of fashion; an exclusive world where you can just walk into VIP clubs because you know important, powerful people. Si was one of an elite few who "owned" London Fashion Week when he was just 21, and had held his position as a well-known designer ever since, working with people like Paris Hilton, Kylie and, of course, most English celebrities.

Even though he was my ticket into the "fashion world", I am not exactly Si's best friend these days, as I did cost him quite a bit of money...

I met Si at the London Fashion Week exhibition. A friend from the pub called Richard took me there. Richard was a regular at the pub I used to work, but older, richer and more powerful than most of the others. He always ordered ribs and chips but never drank alcohol. I helped him with some Slovakian translation, and he took me to the exhibition because he knew I loved fashion.

"What? You can get me to the fashion shows?" I said excitedly.

"When you've got money, you get access anywhere you like."

I couldn't believe I was so lucky.

"That's not luck, honey, you belong there. You are a beautiful woman."

"Maybe I will meet Kate Moss."

"Well, I can't promise you that," he laughed.

It took me quite a while to choose the right outfit that morning. In the end, I picked a classic little black dress. I was very excited about the fashion event – seeing all those lovely people and lovely pieces you can't see in the shops yet. I noticed that Richard was introducing me to his friends as his "girlfriend". I told him I wasn't happy about his game. He was an idiot, but I didn't know that at the time. Or I didn't want to, because I only cared about London Fashion Week then!

Backstage, we met a lot of fashion designers: younger ones, older ones, fashion icons, and upcoming stars.

But they all had one thing in common – every single one of them needed sponsors. So when Richard offered to sponsor COLLEX's new collection, everybody agreed I would be their first model. It was all set up so quickly and Si was their first and main designer.

ME! ME! ME! My big break in the fashion world! Maybe I would become the new Kate Moss, after all.

For the next few weeks, I needed to get ready, which meant going to the gym, dieting, all kinds of beauty treatments, and, most important of all, getting ready psychologically...

I left my day job, doing bookings at the agency, as the dream of becoming the main lady for COLLEX took over everything around me, and I spent most of my evenings with Alisha, looking through the magazines, checking out all kinds of outfits.

"When you become famous, will you take me to all the movie premieres, especially the ones with Brad Pitt?"

"Of course I will."

"Maybe he will fall in love with you."

"Who?"

"Well, Brad Pitt, who else?"

"Brad Pitt is not my kind of man."

"But if he fell in love with you?"

It was just girly giggles and chatter.

That night, I went to bed a little earlier, as I needed to hit the gym before a meeting with Richard, who had kind of become my manager. He was the one who put together all the meetings and the photo shoot. So he was a kind person in my eyes, for doing all this and investing money in the fashion industry. It was only later on I found out the truth.

Just days before all the stuff with COLLEX was supposed to kick off, Richard's business partner came to see me. He informed me that he had no idea what his partner was playing at, as Richard had no money to sponsor or support the Fashion Week event.

"What the hell?" I said, and then went silent, unable to say a word.

"He is simply lying to all of us and this will end up in a real mess."

He kept repeating that Richard had no money at all; he'd lost everything and was acting like some kind of superman for whatever reason.

I was still shaking when the man left. I took the phone and decided to dial Richard's number, praying for an explanation. His phone was switched off, so I tried his assistant instead, who answered after just one ring.

"Ivana, we've got the first few samples, you will love them! Can you come over for a fitting, please? I heard you're going to the gym and I just need to make sure that everything fits perfectly."

I couldn't stop her, so I just listened to what she had to say about the VIP guests' catering before she put me on hold to answer another call. My mind was racing and when she came back, I told her the truth: "Richard hasn't got any money."

She didn't get it the first time, so I had to repeat it myself several times. I still didn't really get it myself, I was still in shock.

"Ivana, I don't know what you mean. We invested half a million of our own money. Do you know how much a catwalk show costs? We have nothing now. What a waste."

I stayed quiet.

"I do hope you are kidding right now."

Sadly, I wasn't.

I apologised to her, even though it wasn't my fault, I was only trying to explain Richard's lack of money, but she hung up on me. Can't blame her, really.

After that, everything went wrong.

Richard disappeared and switched his phone off, so no one knew where he was anymore.

Later on, I found out that the modelling contract he'd sorted out for me was a fake. The big agency had never ever heard of me, but they were quite impressed with the quality of the fake document that Richard had produced.

I never really drink alcohol, but I spent the next few evenings with a glass in my hands. Alisha kept me company.

The more I drank, the more I cried. I felt so stupid and guilty that I had caused problems for other people.

"Pull yourself together, woman. Stop crying!" she urged. "You need to go back to work and forget about all this mess. Don't worry, everything will be soon OK."

"I know that, but at this moment right now, I'm in a mess."

It had been all far too good to be true, really.

At the end of the day, maybe this was supposed to happen. Success shouldn't be that easy and perhaps somebody up there thought I should work a little harder for it.

One thing was for sure, I couldn't just stay on the sofa and cry.

\* \* \*

I got a few modelling jobs here and there and even did some work experience at ICE, the top model agency in the world. Thank God I had kept the numbers for some of the models I used to look after. If any of my contacts needed a model, I would sort them out. I also built up my work as a make-up artist and stylist, and slowly started to collect contacts and meet the right people.

I lived from one day to another, but I had enough work to keep me busy. I was meeting more and more people who were really nice, and my diary was getting filled with all their names. I started working with people, including extraordinary designers whose work could only be worn by a "controversial girl". I also kept doing the make-up for shoots and the makeover studios as well.

I had a good life in London, going to cool parties and wearing fantastic clothes. Sure, I wasn't Kate Moss or even Victoria Beckham (although at that time, I didn't really want to look like her). I was a long way down from their lofty position in the fashion world but I liked my life, even if it was a little bit different and perhaps strange to others.

# 5

# Dating Englishmen

No other man before John had treated me in that way — the way that you treat someone when you really care about them. I had never known what it felt like to have someone who worried about you and made you feel special, who loved you just the way you are.

My first English boyfriend was called James. He looked just like James Blunt and was a first-class player. In fact, he slept with anything that moved! All the women loved him; there was something about him. Women couldn't help themselves, including me.

I was a joke. I stuck with him for four years, during which time I kidded myself that one day he'd change, but our relationship turned bad. I would sleep with other people, hoping to hurt James and make him jealous. It was a crazy time in my life and I couldn't imagine life without him.

But then one day, I just left him…

I needed to get away and forget all that crazy obsession — to start somewhere new, where I wouldn't see his face, and that was another reason why I moved to London.

Boyfriends were not really part of my plan when I moved to the capital, but going out so much meant I did meet a lot of men. Actually, when I first met John, I was kind of seeing a Frenchman called Louis. It wasn't really a relationship, I guess.

Louis and I were sleeping together – friends with benefits. It didn't really have much to do with love really. We were just around "lovely people" from a luxurious world. He loved money and the "good life", as he used to tell me. I soon started to look down on people and separate them into categories, just like him. I became very judgemental, always noticing what clothes and jewellery they wore, as well as their "look". I would even examine their faces to see if they looked after their skin.

I don't think I was happy at this time of my life, but I didn't do much about it. It is very easy to get sucked into that kind of life when you are working with lovely, well-dressed people, and always are around the latest collections, designs and good organic cosmetics. Everything smells lovely and expensive, and all you do is talk about fashion.

In this beautiful blur of fashion and London nightlife, you kind of forget the real world and no longer want to be around people who shop at Tesco and only have a few basic colours in their wardrobe. I think I'd become the kind of person my father had feared I would.

There were three VIP clubs that I would go to – Movida, Maddox and China White.

If you love to go to places like this, you either need to know a few people who work there or be rich or famous. I was lucky to know a few of the promoters and managers at that time, so I never missed the unmissable important parties and events.

These clubs were often used for all kinds of different events, like fashion shows, movies etc., so there was always something "important" going on. There were always photographers around, as well as upcoming models, actors, and people trying to make it in the business, and, of course, the people who had already made it. Sometimes, the children of famous people would come with their friends to enjoy the London scene.

There were also escort girls, who were sometimes quite difficult to spot, as most of them were very well dressed. You would always see them around rich Arabs and they didn't even try to hide who they were. There were a lot of Arabs who had at least three girls around them each night.

You could easily spot all this kind of stuff going on, especially in the toilets, but you just didn't talk about it. The minimum spend on a table for a night was £500, and even a bottle of water would cost the equivalent of the weekly food shop of a Slovakian family.

I went to network and meet the right people at the right time. This was the only reason I would give up my beauty sleep. I am not a fan of overcrowded places, I don't really drink alcohol and do not dance. In fact, I am a terrible dancer. All I was interested in was doing the work that I loved, and I was going to do anything I could in order to get where I wanted to be. I wanted more than I had and used every single opportunity that came along to make that happen. I was desperate to become one of those people on TOP.

I didn't sleep much back then and I was always carrying a huge make-up box across the city, or modelling for upcoming fashion designers. It was quite a hectic life, as I always needed to look stylish and happy.

In the middle of all this, there was this cute, sophisticated, well-dressed French businessman called Louis. Everything about him smelled expensive. After we met at one of the club nights, we started seeing each other when he was in London from time to time. He took me to fancy places and bought me fancy presents. I'd never had a man like him before. He wasn't the kind of guy that you could talk about your problems to. In fact, he didn't really care about my health or whether I was eating enough. Somehow, that wasn't important to me. It was all part of the "perfect", messy life that I lived. We had fun and I had a huge crush on him. Frenchy was the kind of man you would easily fell in love with, but the way he treated women meant that he was not really marriage material, which suited me fine.

Then I met this black guy called John. He looked a bit like 50 Cent, and as though he lived in the gym. I'll never forget the day that I met him for the very first time.

It was early Saturday evening and I was starving. My shoulder was killing me, as I had been carrying my heavy make-up box all way from Hammersmith to Stratford and back. Alisha was at her mum's for the weekend, so I was all alone. I was planning my evening in my head – first, I needed to stop at McDonald's then have a lovely bubble bath and watch some DVDs, and maybe even chat to my Frenchman, if he was online.

I went to McDonald's, put down my make-up box and stared at the menu boards.

"What are you carrying around in this box?" someone asked. "You don't look like a mechanic to me."

I turned around to see a tall, handsome black man next to me.

"Well, you don't look like you work for the FBI either," I joked.

His friend laughed. I pushed my make-up box towards the counter and then ordered a blueberry muffin and cappuccino.

Then I realised I could be in trouble, with hot coffee in one hand, a muffin in the other, and a stupidly heavy make-up box on the floor. To make matters worse, I also had seven-inch high heels.

Focus woman, don't lose your balance.

"Maybe I can help you with that, beautiful mechanic lady?" asked the black man with beautiful eyes.

"I am not a mechanic."

"Maybe you're not, but you are beautiful."

I felt myself go red, from top to bottom. My cheeks were burning.

He took my make-up box and asked me where I was heading. As both of them were walking in the same direction as me, they escorted me home. On my doorstep, I politely said thank you and goodbye. He didn't ask for my number, which was disappointing. I wondered if I was losing my looks, but it didn't really matter because I was home. Finally. I had endured the longest day ever at the studio and I was exhausted. My whole body was in pain.

I kicked my high heels off, put the music channel on and chilled on the sofa, stuffing my face with my muffin. My Frenchman was offline, so I decided to take a hot bubble bath with a Jay Sean CD on – my chill-out music in those days.

I had no idea how long I was in the tub but when I woke up, the water was freezing cold, the CD had finished and I was shaking.

I wrapped myself in a nice, warm dressing gown, and on my way to bed, grabbed my phone and laptop. It was 3a.m.

# 6

## A Visitor

The doorbell woke me, but I couldn't get up. It felt like I'd only just gone to sleep a minute ago.

Then it stopped.

And then it rang again, on a Sunday.

I grabbed my dressing gown and made it down the stairs, thinking that maybe Alisha had come back earlier than planned and forgotten her keys or something.

"Wow, girl, you still sleeping? It's afternoon!"

I froze.

It was the cute black guy from yesterday and I looked terrible! No make-up and I hadn't even brushed my hair or teeth. Damn it!

"Hi," I said, finally managing to pull myself together.

"I was just passing by, so I thought I'd stop to ask for your number."

"What do you need my number for?"

"Well, you never know, I might need a mechanic someday," he smiled.

"I am not a mechanic, you know that."

"I forgot," he said, still smiling.

For a minute or two, we just stood there and stared at each other; it was a little bit embarrassing. I gave him my number in the end and he wrote it down carefully. Then I said goodbye and he left.

I closed the door and looked in the mirror. If this guy calls, he must have a problem with his eyes, I thought to myself.

\* \* \*

The next day, my phone rang; just minutes after I had found out that Frenchy was offline again.

"Hello?"

"John here."

"John?"

"Yes, John."

"John who?"

"The one who helps mechanics with their boxes."

"Ahh, has something broken down then?" I smiled.

"Yes, my plans later."

"That's not good."

"Can you help me out then?"

"I don't think so…"

"I do believe that coffee and a blueberry muffin might help."

Smart, this one, I thought.

"I don't know."

"I am outside your house, now move your ass then."

"Move your ass?"

"Yes, that cute one."

I didn't have any plans and I could really do with a blueberry muffin, so I was ready in five minutes. We spent the rest of the day walking around London. Even though it was autumn, it wasn't really that cold yet. The streets were full of tourists, their hands full of plastic bags and souvenirs.

I did enjoy his company and felt like I'd known him for years. I had never laughed and giggled that much in my life.

We had a good day. Maybe I talked a little bit too much. He didn't mind a bit of window shopping, and we had some more coffee, with chocolate this time. Then he bought me a hat, as I didn't have any and it was getting colder. I do not normally wear hats, as I always look silly in them and they don't suit me at all. Nonetheless, I let him buy me one.

He walked me back home.

"Are you seeing anyone?" he asked me, just when I was looking for my keys.

I shrugged my shoulders. "I don't know if I am, kind of, not really sure what's going on right now." I'd had no contact with Frenchy for a few days.

He didn't smile this time and just stared at me, waiting for me to explain. Well, I didn't feel like explaining anything to anyone.

"Goodnight then," he said, and lifted his hand to wave.

"Thanks for taking me out. I had a lovely day," I said, as he turned to leave

As the door behind me closed, I walked into Alisha. She was right there, behind the door.

"Cute black bodyguard, yes?" she said, putting her hands on her hips.

"He might be a bodyguard, but not mine," I giggled.

"So what is he then?"

"No one. A friend."

Alisha was clearly not convinced, but let it go. We sat down on the sofa and caught up on each other's weekends.

Later that evening, I turned on my laptop to find a message from Frenchy: an invitation to a weekend in Luxembourg, next weekend. I checked my diary, made a few calls to swap a few things around, and wrote back, "Looking forward to it, babes."

I was attracted to John, of course, but I already had something going with Frenchy. John still stopped by sometimes when he happened to be nearby. He was great company and a good laugh. But my head those days was full of the fashion world and my heart was full of the glamorous, sophisticated, designer-clad Frenchman.

John wasn't in luck; my Luxembourg weekend was simply perfect. One of those lazy weekends, but a special one that I'll never forget. Beautiful city, lovely company, and a lot of time spent in bed…

\* \* \*

When I got back to London, Alisha was waiting at the airport with a welcome balloon, like she hadn't seen me for bloody months. I love her.

"Don't tell me anything. Judging by the look on your face, you had an amazing time."

On the way back home, I told her all about it, of course.

"I wish he was living in London."

"Why?"

"Because it would be much easier."

"After a while, it would just become a routine, and you don't want that. You don't want a routine with your exotic Frenchy, do you?"

"I do," I said, and stared at her for a minute. "Yes, I do. Ah well, everything in my life is a little bit complicated."

I was just sitting and rubbing my new Cavalli jumper that Frenchy had bought me. It was so nice and soft.

"Guess who showed up twice, looking for you?"

"Who?"

"Ah, that cute guy you were out with last Sunday."

"John?"

"Oh, he's got a name then?" She started to laugh. "I thought he was a nobody."

"Well, he is."

"Well, he looked good and he's funny."

"What did you tell him?"

"That you were in Luxembourg with a boyfriend."

"Really, that's what you told him?"

"Yes, why is there a problem?" she said, staring at me with a cheeky smile.

"No, not at all."

"OK then."

"And do you know what he wanted?"

"I think he might be looking to become your boyfriend."

"Bad luck then."

"That's what I told him too."

"You are kidding? You talked to him about it?"

"Uhhhhmmm."

"Why?"

"Because the doorbell would never have stopped unless I had answered."

"Well, he is a friend, so he can come around anytime."

Alisha was clearly having fun watching me squirm.

"I thought he was a nobody, but now you say he's a friend?"

"Yes, but…"

"I told him that you are interested in a different kind of man."

I was laughing now too. "Are you crazy?"

"And? It's true, isn't it?"

I was still laughing. "Of course I am. He looks just like an American rapper. So, what did he say?"

"Nothing, he ignored me."

Alisha parked her car outside our house. As she was helping me with my bags from duty-free, one of them fell on the floor and a black baseball cap with gold designer writing on it came out. Alisha picked the cap up. We just looked at each other and smiled.

"I think rappers wear a little bit more colour than this…"

# 7

## *Prejudice*

John became my shadow. More often than not, he just happened to be in the same place at the same time as me – at the tube, park, coffee shop or supermarket. Sometimes, he had a blueberry muffin for me, and he always helped with my bags. During the long, lonely nights when Frenchy was offline, I would think of John. My feelings were definitely getting confused. As much as it's nice to have a man to take you to fancy places and buy you designer clothes, you have to appreciate the man who helps you to carry your bags and turns up with a coffee in hand. It was always nice to see him. When he didn't show up for three or four days, I started to miss him.

He happened to find me in my favourite coffee shop a few times. I would usually be reading a magazine or just checking what events were happening in London that could be good for networking.

"Yesterday, I missed some fun. Sapphire Amy had a little fight with the security guards," I was telling John over a coffee, only a few days before my birthday.

"Who is she?"

"A model. Only a few days ago, I was assisting on her shoot. It was a cool job."

He picked up the magazine and said, "You look better than her."

I smiled. "No, I don't."

"Yes, you do. Only you're very skinny."

"Nobody asked you for your opinion, you know!"

"You get so angry, just because someone tells you that you should eat more?"

"Of course. It is my business what I eat."

"OK."

"OK?"

"OK."

After that, I saw him a few times at the tube but he didn't notice me as the tube was so packed. I only saw him through the space between people stacked inside the carriage. He was dressed up from top to the bottom in a sporty designer outfit, and with his perfect body, he looked so untouchable.

I was kind of getting used to his surprise visits, so I did get little bit upset when he didn't even notice me. I reasoned that I wasn't really looking like my normal self and was wearing sunglasses, but then I do most of the time. They are my must-haves!

One day, he showed up at the tube station once again. I'd had a crazy, busy day at the studio, so it was quite nice to see him. Of course, he helped me with my big make-up bag and we found two free seats on the tube. I was so tired, I used his arm to rest my head on.

"Are you going to the club tonight?" he asked.

I just nodded with my eyes closed. I knew that I would be probably be asleep by the time we got home. Then, this annoying woman's voice woke me up. It was not just her voice, but her language – she was very clearly Slovakian.

"Oh my God, what kind of country is this? Look at this pretty girl with this black man," she said in Slovakian.

I opened my eyes to see a mother and daughter sitting opposite us. I was wearing sunglasses, so they might not have seen that I was looking straight at them. I let my head rest on John's shoulder and listened to their nonsense.

"Such a lovely girl and with this man."

Her daughter just stared outside the window, which was strange because it was a tube train and so she couldn't see anything. I think she didn't want to look at her mother, although she nodded.

"I don't think I will be able to sleep at all tonight after seeing this. I will have no sleep," she was still going on. "This is the end of the world, you know."

I moved a little, as I was giggling quietly.

"Are you OK? Do you understand them?"

I nodded again. "I'll tell you later."

"Tell me now."

"No, no, later."

I was getting kind of used to people staring at us, but this Slovakian woman was really getting overexcited about it. So, I thought, let's spice this up a little for her, so she has something to talk about with her friends back home.

Slowly, I put my hand on John's knee and slowly rubbed forward to his thighs and a little bit higher… he didn't know what was going on but played along.

The Slovakian mother seemed to have breathing problems. "Oh my God, can you see this? No shame at all! If only her mother could see her. And you wanted to stay here! I would die worrying about you!"

John gave me a kiss on my hair. I don't know why, maybe he felt that I was fighting with my own people. After that kiss, the lady and her daughter got off at the next stop, even though the daughter was trying to tell her mother that it wasn't their stop yet. John was pretty pleased too.

\* \* \*

I was looking forward to my 25th birthday and had booked a table at Movida. My life in London was going well. I wasn't a rich, top model, but I was doing a little bit of modelling, as well as make-up for a makeover studio. I was also meeting lots of young people and having a great time.

All day, I received messages on Facebook and texts. My parents and brother called too. Frenchy had promised he would be in London for my birthday and would stay for a few days as well.

Alisha got up early to get us some blueberry muffins and coffee.

"Happy birthday! You up already?" she said, as I came down stairs.

"Yes, I am up, enjoying my birthday morning."

"Enjoy it, maybe it will be your last birthday without a man."

"I've got a man," I protested.

Alisha laughed.

"Alisha!"

"I have to go now, see you."

John popped around in the early evening with some flowers and grapes. We were in the middle of getting ready for our big night out, so our living room looked just like a makeover studio. There was a massive mirror in the middle and tons of make-up all over the place, including lipsticks, foundations and brushes. There were also discarded pairs of shoes all over the sofa and nowhere to sit. I was wearing a beautiful dress by a lovely friend of mine, the designer Pascal Gage. I had done my make-up and Alisha was now trying to fix my hair.

"Well, those posh guys will be all over you ladies," John joked. "Happy birthday, beautiful," he said, giving me a kiss on the cheek.

"Thank you so much, John."

Alisha brought me a second Martini – which I knew was a bad idea; because I eat very little, I get drunk very quickly – and handed one to John.

"To a great evening," toasted John, raising his glass up. Just then, my laptop made a noise.

Frenchy had sent me a message, saying that he was very sorry but his plans had changed. I hadn't heard from him all day. I'd tried to get hold of him, but nothing. Now this!

"How come? I thought you had arrived in London yesterday?" I messaged back.

"I didn't. Change of plans. Lots of work to do. You know how it is."

"It's my birthday."

"I know, happy birthday. Where are you going? Maddox?"

"No, Movida."

"Have a great time. Speak soon."

Before I noticed, John had gone, my make-up was ruined and tears were pouring down my face.

"Can you give me another Martini, please?" I looked at Alisha, who poured me another drink without saying a word. Frenchy had let me down big time.

When we left an hour later, I wasn't in a party mood at all. It was supposed to be such a special night to celebrate my life in London and have fun with my friends. I'd come so far from that village in Slovakia, but I just wasn't in the mood. Also, half of my guests didn't get into the club because they weren't wearing the right outfits, even though they knew how strict the VIP clubs could be. ☹

I drank until the morning and didn't even care what I was drinking. The last thing I remember was someone shouting, "Oh my God – sunrise!"

* * *

The next morning, well, lunchtime really, I woke up still wearing my lovely outfit from Pascal to find an empty house, as Alisha had already gone to her mum's. I felt crap: I had a headache, a weak body and red eyes.

I managed to get to the kitchen and fixed myself a really strong coffee with tons of sugar, forcing myself to eat some cereal with skinny milk. Even with my eating issues, I knew I needed some kind of food or I would collapse.

As I forced the cereal down, I tried to put some pieces of my birthday night together, but there wasn't much I could remember. It was like a blackout. I felt sick, unhappy and useless.

In this strange moment, I decided to check my emails, looking for some kind of apology from Frenchy. There was a big, fat nothing, just a few messages from friends who'd had fun the previous night.

Tears were pouring down my cheeks again. I felt so lonely. The doorbell rang. I couldn't face anybody, but it went on and on, and my headache could take no more.

"Hi beautiful," John said, full of energy. "You're not answering your phone today, so I was getting a little bit worried about you."

"I am OK."

He came into the hallway and started to take his shoes off.

"Did you just wake up?"

"Yes."

"Did you eat anything at all?"

"And who are you? My mum?"

He didn't answer, just looked at me and went into the kitchen.

"I had some cereal," I said, as I walked slowly behind him, "and ate the whole bowl."

"That's all you've eaten? Girl, it's seven in the evening."

"I was sleeping."

"So, you can't be hungry?"

"I will have another coffee then."

"Coffee is not enough – look at you, you're so skinny."

Oh, here they come. Some more tears flow from my eyes. I wanted to stop crying but I couldn't control it.

*Not now. Please, not now, I don't need any of your lessons about eating. Don't be horrible today, I don't have the energy to protect myself to make my point.*

*I've had enough of everything! And this headache is not going away.*

He put some bread in the toaster, looked at me with that soft, kind look in his eyes. Maybe he could see that I was suffering.

He left everything, came closer to me, and, for the first time, gave me a hug. He held me so tight, stroked my hair and whispered into my ear, "I am just worried about you…"

He left after I had eaten my toast and I went to bed.

\* \* \*

My stylish and elegant Frenchman broke up with me in quite a stylish and elegant way too.

A few days later, I got an email. He had been in London for my birthday but wasn't alone. He had company and apparently now, it was more than friendship. If that wasn't bad enough, he decided to point out some of my bad features. He didn't think he could ever have loved me and, of course, didn't forget to mention that I didn't behave like an English lady – whatever that meant!

What a prick!

Staring at the computer screen, I felt so hurt. It wasn't your classic heartbreak; it was more an anger and deep sadness from realising that "my perfect Frenchman" was not actually that perfect at all. He had seemed the perfect man in my head that every woman dreams about – or not!

I poured a glass of wine, wrapped myself up in a cosy blanket and typed "Fuck you!", wondering whether I had the courage to send it, when John interrupted my misery.

"Hi, I was just passing by…" he said, with a smile.

"So why have you got a Chinese in your hands then?" I cut him off.

He smiled again. "Are you OK?"

"No, I am not." I wrapped myself tighter into my blanket.

"You drinking?" he asked with raised eyebrows, when he saw an open bottle and glass next to me.

I nodded.

"Bad news?"

I shrugged my shoulders. "We broke up. My Frenchman broke up with me."

He didn't make any comment, just nodded and walked into the kitchen. I heard him get plates and glasses out of the cupboards. He came back in with plates of Chinese.

"Now eat."

I did.

After that, he made a cup of tea and pulled a blueberry muffin out of his bag. We watched a movie; I don't remember which one. The important thing is that we were sitting very close to each other, much closer than usual.

We later put on some music and chatted about our dreams – well, mostly about mine. I told him that I wanted to be a successful model, and even scouted new faces myself.

He had this gentle look in his eyes and was stroking my hair, then my hands, and then my legs. We spent the whole night together. Well, I mean together.

He was very sweet, cute and gentle. The way he smelled, the way he touched me, the way he smiled, and the way he looked at me. How the hell had I never noticed these things before? He had been around for months.

\* \* \*

Alisha was back from her mum's in the morning and she just looked at me; she didn't need an explanation. She didn't seem at all surprised by the news. To be honest, I was very sore, but these are details I will keep to myself. Let's just say, once you try black, you never go back! ☺

# 8

## The Party

I have to mention one incident that happened to me around this time that might be connected to what happened to me later. It might, it might not. Either way, I did end up in prison, and even today, I am still trying to figure out who might have been behind that – or who tried to put me in the shit.

It was the weekend and Alisha was at her mum's again. I had come back late from work, so I went straight to bed. I had to be up early as I had a photo shoot the next day, and then I would be looking after some models. I woke up to the sound of shouting and mad laughing. I could hear English people giggling and slagging off someone. I looked at my phone to see what time it was: 3a.m. Then I realised that the noise was coming from my living room. Wide awake, I ran downstairs, shouting, "What the hell are you doing?"

As I entered the lounge, I saw a group who had made themselves at home in my house!

Horrible, thick cigarette smoke filled the air, open bottles of all kinds of alcohol covered my table, and I couldn't miss the white lines all over my beautiful, massive mirror.

Everybody went quiet now and all their faces stared at me.

The only person I recognised was Jeremy. He was a photographer that only worked with really elite customers. A few months ago, I had let him stay on our sofa while his place was being decorated, and he obviously still had a key.

"Ivana," he said, opening his arms, "I thought you weren't at home. Alisha is in Southampton, isn't she?"

"So what if she is in Southampton? You think that it's OK for you to just let yourself in and have a party here?"

"It's fun!"

"This is not a club, Jeremy!"

"Come on, just chill with us. We are talking about that new show, that new fashion show on TV, you know this—"

"Get the hell out of here, before I call the police, now!" I wasn't sure where I had got the balls to be so direct, but I made my point. I'm usually so careful with contacts and try to keep everyone happy, but I was so tired and pissed off. I wasn't even thinking about the damage he could do to me professionally.

They left, but I couldn't possibly go back to sleep after all that, and I had to clean up after those pigs.

\* \* \*

"You've got some strange, weird friends in this fashion world of yours," John said, when I told him what had happened the next day. "Strange people with bad behaviour."

I nodded, thinking that there are strange people everywhere really, not just in fashion.

He stroked my hair and gave me a kiss on my forehead.

"That will never happen to you again. I hope we will live together soon."

I went to sleep in his arms that night.

I wasn't sure if I was ready to really move in with John and have a serious relationship, but I could tell he really cared about me, and that was enough for now.

\* \* \*

"I do not know anything about you," I told him the next day, as we walked through the park to the shopping centre. "When I woke up this morning, I looked at you and realised that I don't know anything about you."

He smiled. Obviously, my monologue had made him feel uncomfortable.

"You do know that I make great cranberry tea."

"Of course, and also that you don't take any sugar with your coffee," I giggled. "That's all I know."

He was quiet. You could only hear the snow crunching under our feet.

"I tell you everything about my life, but you don't say much. We talk about me most of the time."

"You are more interesting," he laughed.

"I don't even know where you live."

"That's not important anymore; we will live together soon."

"John, why won't you tell me anything? Don't you trust me?"

"If you really need to know, I will take you there today. I have no problem with that."

"Today?"

"Yes, today."

"OK then."

He took my hand in his and squeezed it, which was his way of ending the conversation.

Then I realised that I might have scared him off, just like the Frenchman. Frenchy had told me in his critical email that I asked far too many personal questions. So, even though I was curious, I didn't ask any more questions.

\* \* \*

Over the next few weeks, our relationship got more serious. I enjoyed spending time with him: cinemas, walks, cuddles, and we even played chess in the evenings. Well, I didn't really play, but I tried to. He was very keen on us moving in together, and I was beginning to get used to the idea. Although, to be honest, I didn't really like the idea of moving out to the suburbs and living with his snoring, his mess and, worse still, losing my freedom. We were having a good time and I had a good feeling about where things were going. He was very supportive and really cared about me. So what if things were moving quickly?

My work diary was already starting to look very busy over the next year. There was a shoot in Turkey and another in Shanghai, and some stuff in London too. I was getting very excited, thinking this was going to be my year, and I didn't want John to get in the way of that! I had put a lot of hard work into getting here and I wasn't going to let anybody try to stop me. Not even him, even though I cared about him. He seemed to understand that I didn't want to discuss this part of my life with him, but then he didn't tell me much about himself either.

He never talked about his bodyguard job, his clients or his family. I had found out that his mum was back home in Africa, his sister was somewhere in London, and his daddy was in New York. I could tell he wasn't comfortable and I didn't want to pry. Instead, I figured that one day, he would talk about it, when he felt ready. I'd leave the ball in his court.

\* \* \*

"Hey John, where did you get this beauty from?" a voice called out, while we were on our way home one snowy January evening. I turned around and saw a little, black man try to run on an icy footpath, which looked funny, as it was very slippery. He was wearing a white jacket, white hat and had big, sparkling, brown eyes

"Hi," said John, with no emotion in his voice – he was not happy, not angry; in fact, there was no emotion at all.

"Lovely to see you," the tiny man carried on. "How are you? What you up to?"

"Just what I always do," John answered, and the little man giggled.

His name was Frank, and from their conversation, I understood that he owned a boutique where I sometimes shopped myself. It sold such lovely clothes. For some reason, I was surprised this man could own a place like that. He just looked weird, and as for his outfit, well…

"Are you really the owner? I love that place," I asked, trying to sound casual.

"Yes, that's my place"

"Oh wow, you do have some great pieces in there, I must say."

"It's our own collection."

"Really?"

"Of course. We create our own lines; design them, make them and then sell them."

"That's fab!"

"Isn't that how it always works?" John asked, looking kind of lost.

I looked at Frank and we both shook our heads.

"Actually, no, it is not. Not with small boutiques like this one. It's quite unique," I explained, glad to talk fashion with someone new.

Frank stood in the middle of the footpath and would not stop talking, like he would happily stay there and chat forever. But it was very cold and I didn't think John was enjoying the conversation about clothes and models. Frank knew the fashion world and mentioned a few names I was aware of. In the end, we exchanged numbers and he told me that I could stop by his boutique anytime I wanted, even after opening hours.

John didn't look very impressed.

Frank called later the same day. We had just got back from viewing a flat in South London. It was a beautiful, quiet area and the flat was small but affordable, and not too far from the tube. That was my main priority.

"Hi Frank, you wouldn't believe how expensive flats are. I don't think I'm going to have much money for clothes anytime soon," I joked.

"I'm not calling about shopping. I want to make you an offer." I turned the TV down and Frank asked me if I would do a photo shoot for his new collection in Buenos Aires.

"It's warm over there at the moment, and most of our clothes are made there too."

"Oh my God!"

"Is that something that you'd be interested in?"

"Of course!"

"Can we meet up then?"

I checked my diary, but the next few days were busy all day, every day.

"We can meet up right now, if you don't mind?"

"OK, no problem," he laughed. "Come over to the boutique."


We came to an agreement about what I would be paid and he also said I could keep one of the outfits after the shoot, which was nice. I would spend 11 days in Buenos Aries, just after Christmas. London was very cold and it would be nice to get some sunshine in Argentina. I hoped I would get a tan (I would more likely go red). It was a chance to see a new country, experience a new culture, and I would become the new face for their catalogue, which would soon be in lots of hands. I was far too excited, just like a little kid.

Alisha was also excited for me.

Pascal, who I always share my news with, was so kind and offered a few cocktail dresses to take with me. Even my mum was very excited. Only John was unexcited, and I couldn't work out why.

"Don't go." He looked at me with sad eyes.

"John," I replied, with a look that said "Don't you dare start now."

"I don't want to be without you."

"It's only a few days and then I'll be back."

"It's two weeks."

"It's a job."

He looked just like a kid who'd had his favourite toy snatched away.

"I am just worried."

I shook my head. I don't know why, but Frenchy came into my head. He would have been supportive of this kind of thing. He wanted me to get famous and make good money. So, what was John's problem? If he was going to make a scene about every job I got then we wouldn't stay together.

He could tell I was pissed off, and cheered me up by looking up a few words in a Slovak dictionary and trying to speak the language. This, of course, made me fall about laughing.

\* \* \*

I was completely exhausted and so lost in my modelling work, I didn't even realise how annoying and unprofessional Frank was. After the business deal was agreed, he called every day, sometimes twice. He also asked me to dinner a few times. The one time I went, I took John with me. I don't think Frank liked it very much, although he never said a word about it. He also sent me flowers a few times and often complimented me on my looks, which seemed a bit strange as he had a wife and kids at home. John was still not that keen on Frank, and looking back, it's easy to see why.

"Would you be my valentine?" he asked one time, and it was clear that Frank's calls had become too frequent and he was taking things too far.

"What are you talking about, Frank?"

"Oh man, I was just kidding, honey."

"I don't get it. I think Valentine's Day is about love. You do know that, don't you?"

"Of course I do."

"I am with John and I believe you should be having dinner with your wife."

I hung up the phone and my whole body shook. Yuck!

John came over later with some lovely flowers and gave me a kiss. He then served me dinner and gave me my favourite dessert – tiramisu.

We were having a lovely evening when John's phone rang. It seemed strange, as people normally didn't call him that late in the evening. John answered it and, looking serious, said, "I will come over."

Apparently, it was work.

"Please don't be upset," he told me. "I will be back in two hours, I promise you."

So I made the best of it, put on my favourite movie, *The Devil Wears Prada*, and ate the whole of my tiramisu.

I woke up in the early hours, as he came to bed.

"Are you angry?"

I shook my head.

"My friend's wife drinks far too much sometimes. She caused problems at the club and then got lost in the streets. We've been looking for her."

"Ah, and he couldn't look for her alone?"

"No. He's got a little baby at home. His neighbour looked after it while we searched for her. It's faster to cover the ground with two men."

I was quiet. I didn't know what to say.

"Did you find her then?"

"Yes."

"And is she OK?"

"Well, not really, but she's alive."

\* \* \*

John started sneezing around lunchtime, a fever developed in the early evening, and he later lost his voice.

"Clever man, running around the city at night," I said, passing him a cup of herbal tea.

"Stay and look after me, I'm ill."

"Nice try, mister, but I'm all packed, the taxi's booked and tomorrow morning, I'm off to Argentina. I'm so excited, there's nothing you can say that will stop me."

"Shame," he said, looking sorry for himself.

If he'd been more important than work to me at that time then lots of things would be very different right now.

Early the next morning, I had my last blueberry muffin for a whole year.

# 9

## Arriving in Buenos Aires

I couldn't find the shower in my hotel room, so I complained to the man at reception, who just stared at me. He then tried to explain that every single room had a shower, before coming up and showing me where it was.

"See?" he said angrily, pointing at the little ball sticking out from the wall, right on top of the toilet.

"Thank you, sir!" I shouted behind him, while I tried to figure out how I could use a shower like this. There was no basin, so water sprayed all over the place. Buenos Aires would take some getting used to.

It proved to be a beautiful place. Here I was, in the middle of a city full of tourists. I was very excited about exploring the place and spent any free time I had before photo shoots walking around San Telmo, enjoying lovely coffee shops, bookstores, antique shops and squares that held the city's famous Sunday markets. I loved Buenos Aires and its culture. I wanted to see everything and enjoyed all the beautiful parks, churches and museums I found.

I once got lost in a very poor, dirty-looking area. The taxi driver told me later that I shouldn't go into these parts of the city alone, and added that I should be very happy to be alive.

Alexie, an American photographer, was in charge of the shoot and the catalogue. His assistant, Anthony, was Frank's friend from Nigeria. He was quite stern and would often have a go at the make-up artists if he didn't like their work, even though they both looked very stylish and professional, and seemed to know what they were doing.

Alexie was quick and very organised. He had planned everything, and so had me doing something different every day. He always knew the best time to get the right light. Thanks to him, I never got burnt, as I didn't have to be out for long, and the make-up artists always covered me up with the highest sun protector.

The photo shoots were organised all over the city. Most of them were set up indoors, although we did have one shoot on the beach, which was great fun. I preferred it when the shoots started really early, so I wouldn't have to work in the worst heat of the day. The clothes weren't as glam as I'd expected, but there were also some really nice pieces. I fell in love with a yellow, open-backed maxi dress that made me feel like an Egyptian princess every time I wore it.

"You're very beautiful; do you get lots of jobs back in London?" Alexie asked me before a shoot.

"Well, I don't do too badly, actually. To be honest, I work a little bit more than Kate Moss, but for much less money."

Alexie smiled. "I think she had to work very hard too, you know! Can you move slightly to the right, I want to try this angle."

I nodded and moved.

"I will see what this year brings. Right now, I do more make-up than modelling."

"You're young. Just take every job and opportunity you can and eventually, you will get there."

"That's exactly how I feel about life; only I hope my boyfriend will feel the same way too. He doesn't seem to like the fact that I am involved in this fashion world."

Alexie made a funny face and nodded, as if he knew exactly what I was talking about.

\* \* \*

I felt a little bit guilty that John wasn't feeling any better back home. He had developed some kind of throat infection and couldn't eat or talk much. I called him on the last day of the shoot and he was in hospital, so couldn't say much. He'd had a fever for the last eight days and was not getting any better. Before John hung up, he managed to wish me a good day and said, "I love you" in Slovak. It brought a tear to my eye. There I was having fun, and he was in hospital on a drip.

I didn't sleep well that night.

"Please God, make sure he is OK. Please do help me and make this relationship work," I prayed.

I was looking for my tiny, little Bible, which was a present from my auntie, Helena. I take that Bible everywhere with me and that night, I actually read it.

\* \* \*

John didn't answer his phone in the morning, which made me even more worried. Staring at my phone wasn't helping, so I went out to get some air and clear my head. I bought a fruit salad and cappuccino and wandered around the city centre for a few hours. I picked up some souvenirs – cigars and exotic chillies for John, grilled apple chocolates for Alisha. The sun was very strong, so my eyes were burning, even with sunglasses on.

I found a bench in the shade at the park nearby, slapped sun protector all over myself and got my book out, *Confessions of a Shopaholic*. It was a book about me, for sure. Occasionally, I looked up to check what was happening around me. There were mums with children and buggies, children with bicycles, loved-up couples, giggling girls, groups of young boys with skaters... just a normal, sunny afternoon in a busy park. A few young skaters were busy chatting, laughing, and showing off on a bench next to me.

I noticed a very weird-looking, young man while I opened one of the chocolates that I had got for Alisha. I was curious to try it and I thought she'd understand. Slowly but surely, this weirdo walked over to my bench, staring at me all the time. For the first time in a very long time, I heard an alarm going off in my head: watch out, watch out! I was trying to focus on my book but was beginning to panic. The next time I lifted my eyes, he was sitting next to me. Seconds later, I realised he had a knife in his hand. He grabbed my right arm and I didn't move, as I was very scared. He was sitting so close to me, nobody could see his knife. If anyone had looked at us, they would have thought we were together. He was talking in Spanish, but I understood only one thing – that he could hurt me. I was trying to speak to him in English, but he squeezed my arm so hard that I screamed out in pain.

One of the boys – the one showing off the most – looked at me, and I whispered, "HELP." A few seconds later, the boys were standing behind the bench and speaking to me in

English. Then they pulled the man off the bench and beat him up. Too much happened in only a few seconds. Thank God nothing had happened to me.

The group of skaters called the police, who didn't speak a word of English, and it didn't look like they cared much either. They just told the boys to warn me that I shouldn't wander around the city alone! Clearly, you can't rely on the Argentinian police to help you.

*  *  *

For the next two days, I was too scared to go out alone, so I hung around with people from the shoot. I could tell from John's voice that he was feeling a little better. I told him what had happened at the park and he went mad.

"What the hell? He probably thought you had lots of money on you."

"Babes, I think he'd have been happy with whatever I had in my wallet."

"Come back home now; it's dangerous over there, do you hear me?!"

"Babes, stop shouting. This kind of stuff could happen even in Hyde Park."

"Good God, I knew I shouldn't have let you go. Come back home, baby."

"It's only two more days and I'll be back with you."

"I will be home. I can leave hospital today."

"Just rest, don't go anywhere."

"I will be home when you come back. Call me, OK?"

"Of course."

We had a goodbye dinner the day before I was due to fly back home. All of us had arroz con pollo – a thick, spicy soup with rice, chicken and vegetables – and then churrasco, the famous Argentinian steak.

"Is everyone still partying at Movida?" Alexie asked me over the meal.

His face was suntanned now, as he'd been out of the city for three days, looking for the Argentinian cowboys – gauchos, apparently. Our make-up artist whispered her own version of events to me. She had seen him with the beautiful wife of a rich Argentinian man.

"Really?"

"Yes, he always meets her when he's here, and sometimes in New York, when she is on a business trip."

"That's funny, to risk being seen like this."

"Risky for him or for her?" She started to laugh and cut into her massive steak.

I looked at Alexie. "Yes, Movida is still a cool place to be, as well as Maddox and China White."

"I have been there a few times; don't remember much of it though."

Everybody started to laugh.

In this business, you have to laugh at people's jokes, even when they are not funny. Alexie wasn't funny at all, but he made sure that people knew he was important, and got all the attention.

I was about to leave and say goodbye to everyone when Anthony stopped me. He shook my hand and passed me a bag of wrapped presents.

"I have some presents here for Frank. I haven't seen him in years and Christmas has only just gone, so I thought I'd get him something. Have you got any spare space in your luggage?"

"Of course, not a problem at all," I said, taking his bag.

"We will send the photos straight to Frank and you will get your money during the week." Those were the last words he spoke to me.

Back at my hotel room, I logged into my Facebook page, as I needed to speak to a few people. I checked my emails and considered some of the castings I'd been invited to. There was also a message about China Fashion Week. Interesting...

I emailed my brother, as we were trying to organise a present for Mum's 50th birthday. Then I listened to some music, but not for long, as there was no R & B on the radio. I was getting a headache from all those Spanish ballads, which seemed to have five guitars playing on all of them. I wanted to go home!

I went to sleep quite quickly, with a really good feeling that my life was going in the right direction. This was my last free evening for a long time. For the whole of next year, I wouldn't be able to even turn off the light when I wanted to.

# 10

## The Calm Before the Storm

I am not a morning person and never will be, but it is easier when the weather is beautiful and the sun has just come out.

I had checked in, called John and was having my morning coffee. I couldn't wait; there were only a few hours to go and I would be with him. I felt very lucky to have such a good man to go back home to. Even though I really love travelling, I always feel at home back in England, with its good coffee, muffins, Sunday roasts with Yorkshire pudding and lovely apple pie with custard when it's cold outside. I was dreaming about what I would eat when I got back, as I'd mainly been living on fruit salads and yoghurts on the shoot.

The flight wasn't great, as I had to make a few transfers, and I couldn't sleep, even though I was tired. Whenever one of the children started to cry, it set them all off. At one point, it seemed like they had a competition to see who could cry the longest! The mums tried to calm them down, walking up and down the aisle, while I counted down the hours.

One more stop in Paris and then I'd be back home again in London.

I took an ibuprofen from my handbag, kicked off my shoes, wrapped myself in the blanket and whispered a Lily Allen song to myself – *LDN*.

# 11

# The Beginning of the End

When I arrived in Paris, I was exhausted. All I could hear in my head and ears was children crying and screaming. I desperately needed a coffee and croissant, but more than that, I really, really needed to pee. I had a kidney infection. It always seemed to happen when I changed from warm to cold weather.

I normally never pee on the plane, as I don't like small spaces, but the pressure was getting desperate! After I went to the toilets, I made my way to baggage collection to pick up my bags, and then I had a few hours to kill before my transfer to London. There was only one bag left on the conveyor belt so I grabbed it and went in search of a café.

As I walked to the main glass door, a security man stopped me, asking if he could see my bags.

"Of course," I smiled, and passed him my luggage.

He quickly opened a bag, searching for something, and then picked up the bag from Anthony.

"Can you please come with me?"

"Yes," I said, shrugging my shoulders.

The customs officer closed the luggage and left it next to the office door.

"Is there a problem with my belongings?"

"No, no worries. I just need to check something," he said nicely, and smiled.

He sat me down in the office and I watched what he was doing. He took one of the presents into his hands and started to unwrap it. I was a bit shocked.

"Excuse me, that is a present for someone else. Is it necessary to unwrap it?"

His scissors stopped.

"So, this is not yours then?"

"No, it is from one friend to another."

"What is inside?"

"I don't know," I shrugged my shoulders. "He just told me that it was something for Christmas."

"Hmmmmm." He looked down at the present, shaking his head.

"Is there a problem with that?"

He didn't reply and quickly carried on unwrapping the present.

It was a lovely leather diary, maybe A4 or a little bigger, along with other leather books of various sizes. The customs officer put a knife inside the diary and started cutting...

"What the hell?" I started, but he just gave me this look that said, "You're in trouble, you'd better be quiet." He put the diary on one side and took out a second, smaller one, and started to cut that as well.

Slowly but surely, he kept on cutting, and then suddenly, white powder just poured out. He looked at me and shook his head.

"Ooh-la-la, here it is," he said.

I think I went white because he asked me if I was OK.

"Oh my God!"

"Well, you will need him now."

"I guess this is not sugar."

"How well did you know the people that gave you this delivery?"

"It's a present, not a delivery."

"Did you know them?"

"I was doing a photo shoot, a summer collection for one of the boutiques. The assistant photographer asked me to take this for his friend.

"Oh, a model then?"

"Yes."

"You know that we've seen models get caught up with drugs before…"

I couldn't even think, let alone speak.

"OK," he said, and put a little bit of powder into a test tube. "Now we will see. If it goes blue, it is pure cocaine."

"Are you kidding me, right?"

The white powder turned blue in a second.

I don't really know what happened afterwards, as I can't remember anything, my memory is very foggy. I just remember hearing a big lady sitting next to me with a glass of water, holding my hand and saying something to me in French. I had no idea what she was saying, but her voice was kind and gentle. I closed my eyes. I was exhausted and desperately needed to pee.

A few seconds later, I could hear someone was asking me a question in English, but I wasn't able to answer it. I could hear them, but couldn't get a word out. It was like I was in a coma, totally paralysed, and I couldn't respond.

I really don't know how long it took, maybe it was five minutes, maybe an hour, but finally, I managed to say, "I need the toilet."

"Of course," said the lady, who stood up and walked me all the way to the toilet door. Then she walked me back to the little room. Slowly, the shock was wearing off and I was getting a reality check. *There was cocaine in my bag! Amongst my personal belongings. Oh, Anthony, you bastard!*

I wanted to go home.

The two customs officer came back to interview me again. "So, you didn't really know these people?"

I shook my head. "I saw them for the first time in my life at that photo shoot."

"Do you know their names?"

"Only their first ones and where they might be. You'll find Alexie in New York."

"Well, that's not helpful." He then moved his hand and said something in French.

The lovely lady gave me some water.

"I want to go home," I said, turning to her, but she only shrugged her shoulders. "I have to go. I will miss my London flight."

Somewhere in the back of my mind, I knew that I would miss my connection to London. Mascara was pouring down my face. I did think for a second that maybe this was not really happening, maybe it was a joke, like those you see on those hidden camera TV shows. But when I looked around the little office, there was no camera to be seen.

Three policemen came in, but as everybody was speaking French, I had no idea what they were talking about. Later on, three men in uniform walked in. The first one was a black man, the second, a skinny, young man, and the third, an older man, who looked at me as if I had just killed someone... I wanted to cry. This could have happened to his own daughter. They spoke French for a quite a long time with the customs officer, before the black guy sat next to me.

"I want to go home, I have done nothing wrong," I said.

They all laughed, which meant that they all spoke English, but chose not to.

"I don't think so," said the black guy. "You have to stay with us for a few days."

"With you, where?"

"At the police station."

"A few days?"

"We will see."

The grumpy-looking, older man reminded me that I was in France, and I shouldn't cause them any more problems, as I was in big trouble already.

"I am not trying to give you problems," I whispered. "I do understand, but I've got nothing to do with those bags, and I'll be very grateful when this problem gets sorted."

"You leave that with us now," he said.

I felt a sharp pain in my belly. "Can I go to the toilet, please?"

The customs officer said something in French, and the grumpy policeman told me that I couldn't, as I only went a few minutes ago.

"I need to go again, what's the problem? Why can't I go to the toilet when I need to? You think I want to run away? Where?" I shouted.

I was angry and in pain, scared and confused, but he didn't let me go. He just pulled out his handcuffs instead.

"Is this really necessary? Do I look like a criminal?" I started to cry.

"I am sorry but this is the usual way we do things," he said, passing the handcuffs to the black officer.

I held out my hands. At the end of the day, they were just doing their job. But I really needed the toilet.

When the officer put them on, he looked at my French-manicured, acrylic nails with three small hearts in every corner of each nail and smiled. He wrapped me in my poncho, held on to my shoulder and guided me out of the airport. It was a strange, secret exit that I had never noticed before. Maybe they only used them for criminals. The handcuffs were very small, so every time I moved, my wrists hurt. They'd held me for about five hours at this point.

I laugh now when I think back to those days. I was so naïve, even then, or just silly. I didn't see the reality of what was happening around me. I thought that maybe the police would put me in some kind of hotel, where I could take a shower, and that everything would be cleared up in the morning and I could return to London.

# 12

# *Parisian Jail*

It was a beautiful Paris evening. Everything was so absurd. Paris was still light with magic streets, cute coffee shops, romantic shops, chocolate and cheese… and there I was in handcuffs in the back of a police car. They even used their siren to bypass the traffic jams. I cried the whole way there. The black policeman gave me a tissue when he noticed that I was trying to use my sleeve.

I was shivering, not only from shock and the cold, but also because my kidneys were really hurting me. I was so scared.

"What will happen to me?" I asked the policeman.

He looked at me, and for a second, looked felt sorry for me.

"They will question you."

"When?"

"In the morning."

"And after?"

"After that, we will see."

As soon as we arrived at the grey office, the officer took my handcuffs off and my wrists felt freezing cold and sore

"Can I please get a jumper from my bag? I am really cold."

Another policeman pointed at a blanket on the sofa, saying, "Use this, it will be fine."

I gulped, and was then told that I would stay here for the night and be questioned in morning.

It felt terrible. I was sick to the stomach and really ashamed.

Even in the evening, the office was full of policemen, and they all just stared at me when they walked past. I wished I could hide behind my sunglasses so that I didn't have to see all those disgusted faces staring at me.

I was taken by the black policeman to a colleague, and they both spoke in French and laughed. I stared at the two of them. *What the hell are you laughing at?*

"I will come to pick you up in the morning. I know it is difficult but try to get some sleep. You'll have a hard day tomorrow."

He left me with another policeman, who walked me to the holding cell.

"Can I make a phone call?" I asked, as soon as I got to the police station.

"Yes, you can, if you tell us who you'd like to call."

"I need my diary or mobile, I don't know any numbers off the top of my head."

"Why not? We need the number and full address of the person you'd like to call."

"Oh my God." I held my head in my hands. There was only one number and address that I knew by heart, but I couldn't call them. I didn't want to. I simply couldn't do that to them. Mum and Dad would go crazy. They didn't need to know what kind of mess I'd got myself into.

"I don't know the numbers by heart," I replied again.

"OK then."

"Can you find any other way?"

"We've got our rules, madam."

My luggage and handbag were both in the corner, so all he had to do was reach over to get them.

"I will need to use the toilet, quite often," I told him. "I've got health problems."

"I am just over here, so call me if you need anything," he said, in very good English. The officer then gave me a plastic plate with rice on it and something strange. Wishing me good night, he pushed me inside a cell of around eight people. Everyone turned to look at me. Oh my God, where am I, I thought to myself.

The holding cell was big, cold, dirty and stinky. I was shocked, as I had never seen anything so disgusting and stinky in my entire life. Along the walls were hard benches. I guessed they were used as a bed as well, and most of them were occupied. I walked straight over to a dark corner and sat on a blanket. The food was disgusting too. The smell of the cell went straight under my skin and nails. *Yuck!*

I would have stopped breathing if I could, so I didn't have to smell that nasty shit.

I was scared of breathing in all kinds of illnesses, bacteria and viruses...

As the night went on, there were more and more "roommates", including prostitutes, homeless people who hadn't washed for months, and students who had bought "stuff" on the streets.

Most of the people in the cell had a crazy look in their eyes. They screamed and kicked the doors, cursing non-stop. Policemen walked around and took the piss out of these people, provoking even more cursing. *Is this possible, that the police could behave like this?! That they actually enjoy this?* It was pure madness!

I was sitting, all wrapped up in a blanket, with my legs pushed up close to me, and singing in my head so as not to go mad. I was singing everything I could think of, from English pop to Slovak classics.

I was by now feeling more tired and psychologically washed out than I'd ever been before in my life. There was no chance of sleeping in that hell. It was simply impossible. Tears poured down my face, as I couldn't stop crying, and I was really hungry. I was in pain and needed the toilet again. I really didn't want to shout this out to the policeman, I would rather wet myself, and so walked past all these crazy people.

This was how hell must look. *Oh good God, please don't let me go crazy in here.*

⁂ ⁂ ⁂

The grumpy, old policeman came to pick me up in the morning and asked, "Did you get any sleep at all?"

I shook my head and asked if I could pee. He could probably tell from my crying that I was in pain, because he asked me if I wanted any medication after I came back from the toilet.

"Yes, please," I nodded, and then he led me to a small office. He held my shoulders tightly, as I was very dizzy and couldn't even walk in a straight line

All the policemen I'd met the day before were sitting in there already, speaking French.

They gave me some pills and a glass of water, and then the black officer asked me if I wanted a shower.

"Can I?"

He nodded and then stood right behind me, while I looked for some clean clothes in my bag.

Everything was clean compared to that what I was wearing right now. I tried my best to find something warm, but this was difficult as I had been travelling from hot Argentina. I found jeans and a light jumper. There were no other options really.

The black policeman walked me to a small bathroom.

For the next few minutes, while warm water poured down my body with clean soap, I didn't think of anything. I scrubbed my skin until it went red and washed my hair three times, trying to get the dirt off me. Then I turned the shower onto cold, which was silly as it made my kidneys hurt again.

*Oh God, a lovely cranberry tea like John used to make for me would be nice right now.*

John. He would be worried. Wondering why I haven't been in touch and was not at home.

I dressed quickly and got a shock when I saw myself in the mirror, looking all stressed out, with no make-up. When I came out, the policeman was still waiting outside the door. He walked me back to the office, which was now full of people who were all looking at me. The grumpy one gave me a coffee and told me to sit down.

My diary and mobile were on the desk and my USB was sticking out from their computer, which explained their stares.

The grumpy policeman lit up his cigarette and finally spoke to me in English.

"Well, girl, tell us how you ended up like this?"

"What?"

"Like this!" He lifted his arms in the air and looked around the room.

I was quiet and tears started to roll down my face again.

"Tell us what happened?"

"I already told you."

"Try to tell the truth, maybe?!"

"You think I was lying to you?"

"What I think is not important"

"So why don't you believe me?"

He blew out the smoke from his cigarette and pointed at my belongings.

"Your photos, on your USB."

"Do you even have the right to look at them?"

I wasn't trying to be cheeky, I just wanted to know my rights.

"I believe it is my job," he smiled.

"They are personal photos."

"We saw. Half of them are from different parties."

"I am young, enjoying my life."

"I believe so."

He looked at my diary and started to turn page after page over. I noticed that they had circled some names with a red pen. I didn't see which ones.

"You're a model?"

"Yes."

"Do you know which industry does the most cocaine?"

"This one?"

"Clever girl."

"I know some people use that stuff."

"You see."

"I am not like them. I don't drink or smoke."

"Really?"

He was looking at those pictures very closely.

There was no point telling him that I just carry one glass in my hand all night while I network and rarely get drunk, and normally have to go to work in the morning anyhow.

"If you tell us the truth, the jury will look at your case more kindly."

"Jury?" I nearly screamed.

"Jury. Did you think I would write your answers down and send you back home?"

"I thought..." I tried to catch my breath. "Does this mean that I will not go home today?"

"If you tell us the names of your confederates, you will help us to get closer to the gang who you are working for."

"But I do not work for any gang," I said, starting to cry again.

"So the names..."

"I gave you their names yesterday. One of them was Alexie and the second one was Anthony."

"And the others?"

"The make-up artist was Lola."

"Do they have surnames?"

"I told you. I don't know their surnames."

"Where are they from?"

"The photographer was American and Anthony was Nigerian."

"Who was the cocaine for?"

"I didn't know there was any cocaine in those presents!"

"Who was supposed to get this parcel?"

"Frank, the man who owns the boutique. We were shooting their new collection."

"What is Frank's second name?"

I knew it, as I'd seen his name on the paperwork, so I closed my eyes and concentrated.

"Hold on, I will try to remember…"

"We have got plenty of time, girl."

*Frank, Frank what? It was simple, simple to remember. It didn't sound African.*

"Kenney! Kenney was his second name."

The grumpy policeman smiled at me.

"You see, you clearly know one of your buddies a little better that you have been letting on."

"He is not my buddy." They just wouldn't listen to me. I looked at the nice black policeman, who smiled back.

"Those people in Argentina, did you know them?"

"No. I have never worked with them before."

Grumpy lifted his eyebrows.

"I mean, I have never done any photo shoots with them before."

*Oh God, help me here, please.*

"And this Frank. Frank Kenney?"

"I met him in London."

"Do you have any photos of him?" he asked, pointing to the computer.

I shook my head. "No, we weren't close friends. I only met him recently."

"Where?"

"On the street."

"Where?" he asked again.

"I met him in passing with another friend of mine. He knew my other friend."

"Your friend's friend?"

"Someone he used to know."

"Do you know where from?"

"No, I don't."

"Did your friend ever say anything about him?"

"No, nothing."

"So what happened next?"

"What do you mean, what happened next?"

"He gave you a work proposition?"

"Yes, something like that. He contacted me and asked if I would like to be a face for their new collection."

"And you wanted to."

"Of course, I like my work."

"Was your friend OK with that?"

"He didn't pay any attention to it."

"Do you always work with people you don't know?"

"It is normal in this business."

"Have you got a picture of your friend?"

"No."

"Why? You're not close to him either?"

When he started to ask about John, my throat went dry. I started to cry and could only whisper. John has no idea where I am now, I thought. Oh good God, he must be worried.

I wiped my face with my hands. I was very tired and trying to concentrate on their nasty questions, but it seemed they were trying to trick me. They were looking for an answer that I didn't know. I was sweating now.

"We are close," I sniffed.

"So why don't you have a photo?"

"Because some people don't like their pictures taken."

"Why not?"

"Not my business, I respect that."

"How long have you known him?"

"Since autumn."

"Did he chat you up or...?"

"Are you serious?"

"Answer, girl!"

"I guess. I was seeing someone else when we met."

"So how did he get you then?"

"Excuse me?"

"You heard the question?"

"Well... he was good to me."

"What do you mean by good?"

"He looked after me."

"Financially?"

"No, we are planning to move in together"

"That's quick."

I was quiet, just staring at my beautiful nails. My nails reminded me of my life.

"What does he do for a living?"

"He... is a bodyguard."

"Bodyguard?"

"Yes."

"Can you be clearer?"

I shook my head. "He doesn't talk much about work."

"Is he black?"

"Yes."

"And is Frank Kenney black too?"

"Yes."

The policemen just looked at each other. Then the black policemen wrote something down.

"Do you know his family?"

"No, his father lives in America and his mum's in Africa."

The grumpy policeman went quite for a while.

Then he asked, "Have you had offers for photo shoots outside of England before?"

"Not much. I've got a modelling job coming up in Turkey and a beauty shoot in Shanghai."

"Uhhhmm." Then he went quiet and looked at me. "So you're moving in with a man that you hardly know. He probably has something to do with that photo shoot job and Frank, and you're telling me that you had no idea about the drugs in your bags?"

"I didn't know."

"It's clear that you carried this as a thank you."

"That's not true."

The black policeman said something to him in French, and he lit another cigarette.

I was crying even more now. Why was this man being so nasty? Why was he picking on me, I hadn't done anything wrong! I only tried to work to become successful!

I spent the whole day with them, answering the same questions over again and again. Why? How? Who? Who with? They asked for all the details, even those I didn't remember or didn't know the answer to.

I wanted to scream out, "No! I don't know anything; I have nothing to do with this... I have no idea why I am sitting here!!! Can you leave me alone? Stop staring at my pictures, give me my belongings back and let me go home!"

I was so angry that I couldn't even think straight. I felt angry with everybody, and most of all, angry with myself for being so naïve. I tried to let go of my rage and focus on how I was going to deal with what was happening to me now, and what would happen next, but my mind was going wild all the time.

At the end of a long day, they brought me a baguette and an apple. Then the black policeman escorted me to the car, using handcuffs again. We drove through the city and I recognised some of the most famous streets.

Even though it was cold outside, people were sitting out under lamps, wrapped up in blankets, holding steaming hot cups of coffee. Paris.

\* \* \*

At the court, I took another pill and my kidneys calmed down a little, but everything else was going mad inside me. I was angry, depressed, anxious and sick – all at once. I couldn't understand how this had happened, how I was sitting in a cell, waiting for my court date, without having any idea when I should be back in London. I still hadn't spoken to John and it had been two days now. I knew he'd be going crazy. It wasn't just him, my family would know something was up if I didn't get in touch with them soon. Pascal had asked me to do the make-up for his new fashion show, and some of the models were the ones who I had managed to get work for when I was an agent. God knows how many people must have left me messages.

I wondered how long I would be stuck in there. I once saw a movie about an American girl who got stuck in a Thai prison for seven years. Seven years!

I could feel tears pouring down my face once again. I tried to wipe them, and as I moved my arms, my handcuffs made a noise.

A policeman looked over at me. "Just say you did it." He said this as if it was an inconsequential matter, as if it was nothing – like he was telling me to wear my hair down or up in a ponytail. "If you say you knew about the drugs, it will be much easier to get out of this situation."

I didn't say anything. I felt that he had said everything that he had to say.

I wanted to sleep like I'd never slept before, but instead, spent my second night in a worse place than the holding cell. This time, I was sharing a cell with three Thai girls, who didn't speak any English. Apparently, they had tried to get to London with fake travel documents. They screamed like mad women. Judging by the smell of them, the last time they took a shower was in Thailand, probably a month ago.

I tried so hard to get some sleep, but both the stench and the cold, hard, wooden bench I lay on made it impossible.

When I did close my eyes, I saw the policemen's faces, as well as colours and voices, memories, doubts and remorse. I started to calm myself down but it was very difficult not to cry, and I quickly switched to feeling sorry for myself. I had no idea what would happen to me, but I told myself that things would get sorted and I would go home soon. I didn't really believe that.

I wasn't just a victim of a cocaine gang; I was also a victim of French justice.

And they had no mercy.

# 13

## More Questions

The nice black policeman picked me up from the holding cell in the morning and took me back to the police station for more questions.

"You didn't sleep again?" he asked, passing me a plastic cup of coffee.

"You can tell?" I did try to smile, but I could imagine how I must look right now, and it made me sick to the stomach.

He nodded.

"Who could sleep in this disgusting place?" I said, sipping the hot coffee.

"Finish that, then we need to get moving," he told me.

I drank the nice, warm coffee and then he escorted me to his car.

He turned on his car radio and Chris Brown's *No Air* came on. That was my favourite tune back in those days. I drove John crazy with that song, playing it over and over again. Tears were in my eyes again. I felt so lost.

"I will try to sort it out. You could have some sleep during the day here with us."

"I don't think I will be sleeping at the police station; it's impossible."

When we got to the police station, he took my handcuffs off and called a doctor, who gave me a sleeping pill. Then he brought me a banana, made sure I ate it, and took me to a quiet room, pointing to the sofa. When I woke up, it was already afternoon.

The same difficult policemen, the same questions. I couldn't even think straight. I was exhausted. I felt frozen and somehow distanced from what was happening around me. I was a mess and couldn't really process what was happening to me.

"Sweetheart," the older policeman began, who looked old enough to be already enjoying his pension, "your friend, Anthony, is a real asshole. You clearly have no idea of what kind of mess you are in. I'll tell you how these people work. Your friend has absolutely nothing to do with fashion; he is just a drug-dealer. These guys are not people from the fashion business. They are scumbags and very good actors. They had everything nicely planned, from beginning to end. They had an ugly game plan, and I will guarantee you that your boyfriend had something to do with it."

"I don't believe it!" I answered, feeling very tired.

The policeman shook his head. "Nobody believes it, but when I get proof, you will be surprised. Don't you know that black men are like this?"

"Like what?" I asked, full of rage.

"Especially Nigerians."

"Oh my God, can you hear yourself? Your colleague is black. You can't put all black people together in one category."

I looked at the nice black policeman, who smiled.

What happened next was much too difficult. It was the same stuff, over and over again. Questions. Questions. Questions. The only difference this time was they brought me more food: croissants and McDonald's. I guess I was slimming down right in front of their eyes. I could feel my jeans falling off my hips. I had had two nights in custody and my body was suffering.

That night, they took me back to the holding cell, where I spent two more nights. It was getting predictable. Every night, different foul-smelling people were there, drunk and high from the streets, kicking the door and shouting at the rude and arrogant policemen.

\* \* \*

Friday was my last day at the police station. My trial had been arranged for Saturday. The policeman who gave me my court date told me the fact that I worked in fashion might not impress the judge.

"Not everybody in fashion takes drugs," I argued. "OK, some people do, but that's not my business! Why don't you go to Cannes during the fashion week? French people are so proud of the Film Festival, but there is more cocaine there than you could ever fit in my luggage." When I told him that, he started to laugh.

The cute black police officer came to see me that evening. "Don't worry," he said, as he opened the door. "Everything will be sorted out. You'll probably have to go to prison, but that's not the end of the world, you know."

I do not know what came over me at that moment. Maybe it was because he had been kind to me, but for some reason, I said, "Could you let me go on Facebook for five minutes, please?"

He slammed the door and that was the last time I ever saw him.

# 14

## My Trial

I was given a French lawyer, who told me things would be much better for me if I told them that I knew the drugs were in my bag. It was a lie, of course, I didn't; but my lawyer said I'd be in jail for years unless I said so. So I signed her documents. Having spent just a few days in custody, I knew there was no way I would survive a sentence that lasted for years. I was desperate, so I agreed to play along.

I got to speak to the court, but it was pointless. In their eyes, I was a model, so I must be either taking drugs or dealing in them. All I remember saying was "yes" and "no".

My trial stretched from Saturday to Monday. Compared to the cell in the courthouse, the dirty, stinky holding cell was five stars! The worst part was the stench from the toilets, which were the ones where you stand up on top of a hole in the ground. There was no privacy, with nothing to separate you from the rest of the room.

The cold, stone benches were really uncomfortable, and policemen would sometimes check on me, mostly talking French and laughing. Some of the prisoners were deranged. It was very cold and all my senses were completely messed up. I was trying so hard not to break like some of the others had. Do not go crazy, I told myself, and started to pray. I remembered some of the prayers from my childhood and repeated them over and over again. Then tried to remember the words to my favourite songs to keep my mind occupied.

I probably looked as crazy as the rest of them, reciting the lyrics. So what. I would not let any of them – the crazy assholes, criminals, pervert policemen or anyone else – get to me.

I was sentenced to twenty months in prison and a five-year ban from French territories. There was an extra sting: if I wanted to leave France after that, I would have to pay the French government the value of the drugs found in my bags – 200,000 euros.

# 15

## Arriving at the Prison

I'll never forget arriving at the prison. It was dark and I was exhausted. I couldn't even cry anymore, it was such a surreal, empty feeling. It felt like a five-star hotel at first, compared to the holding cells, but the first few days were absolutely terrible. There was no hope – absolutely nothing to stop me from getting so depressed. When I think about prison now, I can't really describe the hell. It can only be really understood by those who have suffered it themselves. It's brutal.

They place you in limbo with no hope and nothing to look forward to. They won't let you speak to your loved ones about how you feel or what you are going through. The only people you can talk to are the other prisoners, who are mainly crazy or nasty.

The prison guards don't respect you at all. They think you are the dregs of the human race and don't deserve any rights, not even the most basic ones. Everything you are used to gets taken from you as a matter of course. And I do not just mean mobiles and computers. I am talking about silly things, like razors for shaving, body or hand cream, hairbands and even nail clippers.

Every time I found out that there was something else I couldn't have, it felt like a fresh blow, so I became very low at that point.

My cell was small, but I was just glad and very grateful to be alone in there. On the left-hand side was a narrow bunk bed. I couldn't understand how fat women could sleep on it without having an accident. There was also a small TV sticking out from the wall with two or three French channels. Right underneath it was a toilet, which was next to the door. There was also a basic sink and table.

"Try to pull yourself together," my prison psychologist said to me during my initial assessment. "Don't make this messy situation even worse."

"Have you ever been through anything like this yourself?"

"No."

"So how can you give me advice then?" I knew she was trying to help, but I felt frustrated.

"You will not be here forever, remember that."

"I am here for two years, minimum. They want 200,000 euros. Should I start a charity collection because I'll never get that kind of money?"

"If you show good behaviour, you may be able to get a reduced sentence. Also, you can give them some money if you do some work while you are in here. Of course, it won't be much, but it is a sign that you are trying."

"I will never make that kind of money in prison."

"Don't worry. Nobody's ever had to pay the full amount."

I started to cry. "Today is my mum's 50th birthday. She doesn't even know what's happened to me."

"Maybe your family have already found out."

"Oh my God, could you imagine what they would think of me?"

"Don't think about that. Don't try to rescue your family. They have each other. Try to rescue yourself, because you could easily go mad in here. Then you would never leave."

Later on that day, they brought me a pen and paper and I wrote some letters to my parents and brother. I was crying while I tried to explain what had happened, choosing every word very carefully. I was scared that my parents would get sick or even die from shame and embarrassment when they found out where I was.

Not much goes on in their small village in eastern Slovakia. Life is simple and every day is pretty much the same. When I was around 12 years old, I told my mum that I didn't want to live in the village when I grew up. She laughed, not being able to imagine what life outside the village could be like for me. Well, she could laugh now, look at where I was! I didn't know how my parents could deal with the combination of the words "prison" and "daughter". I was getting myself mentally prepared for the possibility they wouldn't want to know me anymore. In my letter, I wrote that I would totally understand if that was the case.

I had to finish my letters in the morning because the lights went out at 7p.m., not coming back on until 6a.m. There was a long, cold night ahead of me.

# 16

## Noticing I Was Gone

Back in London, I was never without the internet or my phone for more than a few hours. Everyone teased me about checking my emails and phone as much as possible. Straight away, the day after I was supposed to have returned from Argentina, people started to worry because they couldn't get hold of me.

The first one was Alisha, who left messages on my answerphone and found it very odd that I wasn't online. She knew me better than anybody else in the world, and contacted some of our friends from Southampton, to see if they'd heard from me. Of course, they hadn't. So she then called my Slovak friend, Anicka, who also lived in London. John was next on her list, but the last time he'd heard from me, I was at Buenos Aires airport. He was sick with worry about where I had disappeared to. Alisha was by now freaking out and eventually called the police to report me missing.

She also rang my brother, who called every embassy he could think of – even the Slovak one in France. The French embassy told him that they couldn't give him any information without my permission, even though they must have known what had happened to me – the judge's decision, everything!

It took the Slovak embassy a total of four months to even bother to visit me. The lady from the embassy came in and sat nicely opposite me, saying sweetly, "I thought you would be going a little bit crazy."

"Excuse me?"

"Well…" She stopped. "You look sedated."

"I've been here for four months now; I have no more energy to show my emotions."

She nodded and took out her paperwork.

"Are they abusing you?"

"NO."

She wrote something on her papers.

"Do you get food?"

"Yes."

She made some ticks and crosses on her document.

"Have you thought about killing yourself?"

"No," I laughed.

She made a cross on her form.

"Do you miss anything?"

"I want to go home. I am innocent."

She started to cough. "You did say you did it."

"Only because I had to in the end."

"Hmmm. You have lived in England quite a long time, is that right?"

"Yes, but I was born in Slovakia."

"You do know I can't really help you."

"I've seen how other embassies have helped some of the women in here."

"I can't help you."

"So why did you come?"

"We could send you some Slovakian magazines if you'd like us to."

"That would be nice," I said, realising this was the best I was going to get out of this woman.

She wrote something down and left. I never received a Slovak magazine from them. They never cared about me.

After her visit, I become even more depressed. The Slovakians would happily let me die in here because I had lived in England for a few years, or because I didn't give the right answers on that bloody form. I contacted the British embassy because I had seen how active they had been with the cases of other women in the prison. But no luck there either. Even after all those years, I had never changed my passport to a British one, so they weren't able to help me either. "Please contact the Slovak embassy," they told me.

Oh well, thank you.

\* \* \*

My parents found out about me from a Slovak undercover policeman. It was about four months after I'd been sentenced and before my letter to them arrived. The policeman knocked on the door and simply asked my parents if they knew where I was.

"She was in Argentina on a photo shoot," Mum told him, "but I think she should be back in London by now."

The policeman told Mum that I was not in London and I would not be for a while. "Your daughter was found with drugs in her suitcase. Nearly three kilos of cocaine."

I can only imagine what kind of shock that must have been for my mum. She would not believe that I would do something like that. She knows me. When the reality sunk in, she wrote me a very supportive letter, in which she said she would pray with dad for my return home. When I read it, I cried the whole night. I was crying a lot during that time, mostly at night, into my small, hard pillow; but during the day, I had to look strong. The women prisoners were no joke, so I simply couldn't afford to show any sign of weakness.

My family told my cousin, Danka, who got in touch straight away. I gave her my Facebook and email logins, and she started contacting the friends who I wanted to know, telling them where I was. I felt a bit stronger now that my friends and family knew I was in prison. I didn't want them to visit though; I didn't want anyone to see me like this. It would be too hard. Life carried on for all of them. All my jobs were given to other models and make-up artists, and my bank account was looking very bad. I was still receiving invitations to the VIP clubs though, which made me laugh. Maybe some people would be surprised that I had stopped coming to the parties. Well, I couldn't, I was sitting in prison, behind bars…

# 17

## Getting to Work

I took the psychologist's advice and started to work in the prison. Otherwise, I thought I would go mad in that tiny room, plus I would score some points and earn a bit of pocket money.

My shift was from 8a.m. to 4p.m. Each morning, I went down to a workshop in the cellar. Our job was mostly stuffing plastic envelopes with promo flyers for a well-known mobile phone company. At first, it didn't seem like a hard job, something a pensioner would do to keep things ticking over. However, I quickly found out why those jobs were done in prison. You could be the most hardworking person ever, but even then, you could not do it for more than two days. After just a few hours, you were brain dead. Your hands were chapped and riddled with paper cuts, and the monotonous routine gave you a headache. Also, if you wanted to make any kind of money, you had to be fast – and I mean very, very fast – while still concentrating and being careful. The work was terrible, but it was much better than doing nothing. There was a kind of companionship with the people there too. I didn't feel so alone and we'd sometimes chat. I worked two full weeks in my first month and my payslip was ten euros and fifteen cents. When I read this, I thought, you have to be kidding me!

When I started, everyone in the workshop just stared at the new face. Matilda, who was a lovely black woman of around 50, took care of me straight away. She told me if I worked very fast and well, they would give me extra work to take into my cell at weekends as well. (I found out later that not everyone got that extra work.)

"Why do I have to work during the weekend?"

"Because you will die in here," she told me, and she was right.

Without filling those envelopes, Saturdays and Sundays were the slowest weekends of my whole life. I thought about John non-stop because I had nothing else to do. Time was going so slowly as it was. I was used to a fast lifestyle. I was always on the go, booking jobs and meeting people. I loved rushing around London with a coffee in one hand and a blueberry muffin in the other. My time here was already beginning to feel like a lifetime.

6:00a.m. Alarm
6:30a.m. Breakfast inside your cell
7:00a.m. Work
12:00p.m. Lunch inside your cell
1:00p.m. Work
5:00p.m. 1 hour to go into the garden and shower
6:00p.m. Dinner inside your cell
7:00p.m. Lights out

From 7p.m. until morning, you are in the dark, alone with your thoughts. It was a depressingly sad time. Sometimes it was very hot, sometimes very cold, and sometimes, you heard people screaming, crying, shouting, and singing some kind of ritual. Madness, pure madness. I was trying my best to do everything I could to get myself tired, so I that I would actually get some sleep. Until the lights went out I mostly read or wrote in my diary. Later on, in the dark, I made up an exercise routine for myself.

In time, I got a little lamp, so I could have some light. Some nights, I would just stare out of the window at the city. I have never felt so lonely ever in my entire life. I even started talking to some of the pictures I had put up on my wall. They were torn out of magazines that a nice woman called Lesley secretly pushed under my door. On particularly bad days, I even thought the pictures were talking back to me.

Every day after work, I returned to my cell with a little bit of hope inside me that there might be a letter waiting for me from my family. My mum wrote letters full of love and support, and tried to cheer me up with some family news. Mum was clearly worried that I might stop eating and give up mentally. Her letters were full of positive energy, but she was always asking me if I had any problems or anyone was giving me trouble. I promised myself that if I ever made it out of here alive, I would return home to my parents straight away. I was very lucky and grateful to my family. I felt very guilty for putting them through this, and I really worried about how my mum was coping.

Alisha wrote as well, and I asked her if she could check my emails and Facebook, as well as Danka, and let me know if anybody asked about me. She did tell most people that I was in hospital with anorexia. Clever girl, as nobody would be surprised if I had a food disorder. A friend from work even wrote back to her with, "ABOUT TIME SHE STARTED TO DO SOMETHING ABOUT IT."

Andrew and Janet, who I had au paired for back in Southampton, wrote too. Andrew wrote, "I always told you – don't trust people, especially when you travel. You only see good things around you; you can't see how bad the world is." He was a sailor, so he knew what he was talking about. He said the children were asking about me and wanted me to come and visit them soon.

My cousin, Danka, wrote too, while Anicka, my Slovakian friend in London, kept me entertained with letters about planning her wedding in the summer. Everyone who knew me kept writing letters, except John. He was the only one who never wrote.

I waited for his letter day after day, waiting for a miracle. Then, after a few months, I gave up. It felt like I was more likely to get a letter from the 50 Cent, and it really hurt. We were about to move in together and now I got nothing! I even started to entertain the thought that the policeman had told me the truth and John had set me up; although, deep inside, I never truly believed it. I knew he wasn't an asshole, but your mind plays tricks with you in prison. A little voice inside my head kept whispering, "Why hasn't he written to me? Why doesn't he care where I am or what's happened to me?"

If you have a broken heart in London, you can go out to Maddox or Movida, where you will find a lot of men to help you get over it. A simple compliment is enough to make you feel better. Then you can go shopping, eat ice cream and chocolate with your girlfriends, and have their support. They will listen to you cry, call your ex a total asshole, and tell you that you can do much better. Here in prison, I had no one.

My cousin, Danka, emailed John. She told him what had happened, where I was, and that she needed money to get me out. He never replied.

# 18

## *Life Stories*

Most of the inmates were African and Arab women, who didn't like each other very much. Many of them were on anti-depressants and sedatives. They looked spaced out and stared blankly, just like zombies. They moved very slowly and couldn't remember what had happened just an hour ago. Some of the more aggressive ones I worked with would suddenly flip, several hours into a shift, claiming that you hadn't said "Good morning" to them, even when you had. They couldn't remember a damn thing.

"You will not make me like them," I told my psychologist when he offered me pills. After a while, he stopped offering them to me.

The worst times were when they ran out of pills – usually when the psychologist was not in at the weekends. They would go really crazy, shouting down the whole building, kicking the doors. At night, you could hear them for hours, until the guards found out what was going on and locked them in the solitary cell.

This "special cell" was downstairs in the cellar. It had no windows and no food. I don't know what went on in that cell, as I never went down there.

I tried to stay away from any conflict with anyone, so I only made friends with very few people – Matilda and Marie, who were in the cells either side of my own, and Lesley, a wild child in her 50s.

Matilda was from Africa but lived in Amsterdam. She had never worked in her life or even finished school. Instead, she made money as a drug-dealer.

She picked someone up at the airport, or gave something to someone, or would sometimes travel. She was sitting in this Paris prison because she had been caught with about sixteen kilos of cocaine on with her – I had only had three on me!

"Sixteen?"

She nodded. "Everything was planned, but someone grassed me up."

When Matilda heard my story, she told me I was stupid to trust those bastards. Apparently, Nigerians cannot be stopped; they will do whatever it takes. She told me they would even use their own children or grandparents as drugs mules.

Despite her cynical outlook, Matilda was always happy and in a good mood, so I really liked spending time with her. She helped me to stay positive.

Once, she found me crying in the garden after I had just seen a clip of the Cannes Festival and recognised some of the models from the London party scene. Frenchy and his friends were there with gorgeous blondes, and I just couldn't bear the gulf that existed between my life and that!

"Forget about it," Matilda said when I tried to explain this to her. "It's thanks to fashion and people like that that you are sitting here now."

"Matilda, do you know what happened to my life?" I said, wiping tears from my eyes. "I will never walk down the catwalk again. My dreams of being in *Vogue* are over.

The best I can hope for is a promotional flyer about drug smuggling!"

Matilda laughed like a mad person. She really couldn't understand what I was so depressed about it.

"Come on, look at that black model, what is her name… Campbell. She went through all kinds of stuff and they are still putting her photos all over the place."

"But…"

"You'll feel better if you put some make-up on. When I look at you now, I can't understand how you used to be a model," she teased

Matilda the only person in the whole prison who wore make-up on a daily basis – mascara, eye shadow and foundation. Many women laughed at her, but she never cared. She didn't worry about any of them. She was a large lady and didn't have a problem with speaking her mind, to anyone.

"How did you cope with the stress of the drugs world?" I asked her once, when we were outside in the garden.

"You get used to it here, sweetie, you get used to it."

"But you knew that you could get caught at any time and go to prison…"

"I made a few thousand euros in a single day for just a few minutes of fear… it was worth it."

She would entertain me with crazy stories about the drug gangs. Some of them sounded so ridiculous that even Hollywood writers couldn't have made them up. She told me about how they would mix cocaine in tinned food, and then boil it to extract the drug. They even put it in baby formula, and somehow managed to iron it into a special fabric, which would again be boiled to get the cocaine out.

They also got people to travel wearing fat suits filled with cocaine, and some of the pilots and air hostesses were even in on it! It all sounded mad to me, and although she was my friend, it was people like her who had put me in here.

"You don't think that this is bad?" I asked her.

"What do you mean?" she replied, giving me a quizzical look.

"Well, drugs are a nasty thing, and you are making money out of poor addicts," I said, hoping I hadn't overstepped the mark. I didn't want to anger her, but I couldn't just act like I was fine with the whole thing.

Matilda thought quietly for a minute, and then said, "You're absolutely right. I must pray more often!"


Lesley used to love listening to Matilda's stories. Lesley was English, and despite being in her 50s, there wasn't anything in life that she wouldn't try. She was wild, adventurous and passionate, and maybe a little bit silly and crazy as well.

She was certainly paying for her crazy lifestyle now. Coming back to London after a trip to Cuba with her new man, she forgot there were a few grams of cocaine in her jacket pocket. Maybe they hadn't had a chance to use it all before they left.

Her daughter was fed up with looking after Matilda, when it should have been the other way round. She'd had enough of her bad behaviour. She was still an amazing daughter, however, and often sent her parcels full of English magazines. Lesley always passed the magazines to me, with funny comments scrawled on everything. She did have her own style and would make some fab fashion comments on the pictures of celebs. I would then write my comments or reply to hers. Swapping these magazines and sharing jokes kept us sane during the long weekends.

Matilda's stories also kept us entertained and Lesley questioned her all the time. Lesley was fascinated by her drugs ring, and one day, asked Matilda how she got caught.

Matilda just pointed to a pack of guard dogs outside the prison. "Their dogs are trained. The airport dogs are really good, but when the security man stopped me, I flirted with him so that he completely forgot who he was." Matilda was laughing so much that her massive boobs were jumping up and down.

Marie was another person that I got quite close to. Her cell was right next to mine, so if I wanted to chat, we signalled by banging a pencil on the radiator. Marie told everybody that she was in prison for drugs, but that was not the case. If some people had known the real story, they might have killed her. It was an unwritten rule in the prison: anyone that hurt children never had any peace. It was not only the prisoners, but also the guards who abided by this rule, so she knew the guards would probably turn a blind eye if someone tried to hurt her. To be honest, we did start to wonder what the truth was, as it was a little bit suspicious that Marie saw a psychologist every single day. Most of us only had an appointment once or sometimes twice a week. Most of the time, she would come back from her session all cried out.

One day in the garden, she couldn't hold it in anymore and told both Matilda and I all about it. She was crying and we both cried with her. She was the first person I had met in custody that I felt comfortable talking to. Her tired face looked stressed out and full of wrinkles. She even had a little bit of grey hair creeping through. Her only misfortune was that she married the wrong man, who didn't deserve her. He was an alcoholic who would beat her daily, and they had no money to live on. He didn't like her to go outside with the children, in case she said something to someone about her beatings. When he got into one of his moods, he would hurt all of them – even the kids. Her little boy was only three years old, and her girl just two.

Her kids were in such a state that one day, they threw up their soup. Marie didn't know how to calm them down anymore, so she made a decision to stop this hell they were living through.

She poisoned her children to give them peace and then herself, while her drunken husband slept in their bedroom. Death was better than the life they were living. Her children died but Marie woke up in hospital and was taken straight to the police station. She spent a whole week in those cells. They didn't give her any food, just water, and didn't let her have a shower. Nobody asked her why she had done it, or asked her what suffering she had gone through. She was only a killer, one that people spat on.

On her third day in the holding cell, she got her period. When she asked for pads, the police laughed at her. So she spent the rest of the week sitting in the same dirty underwear, while she was questioned. Blood was pouring down her legs. Her story made me realise that I hadn't had it too bad.

"What a bastard, I hope he rots in hell," Matilda said when she heard about Marie's cruel husband. I just nodded.

Marie was only waiting in "our" prison for her big trial, and I have no idea what happened to her in the end.

I only knew the rest of the prisoners in passing. One part of the prison was for women from Al-Qaeda. They were apparently here for seven years. Nobody really talked to them. It was better to stay away. I have no idea what a terrorist looks like, but most of the prisoners and guards didn't get involved. They looked scary.

I still don't understand why they had computers in their rooms, and wore short skirts and low-cut tops. During Ramadan, I even saw them carrying bags of food upstairs.

My fringe was getting so long now, it was quite a difficult to work or even see properly without wearing a hairband. My hair had been cut in a "sophisticated bob" before, but it was now just a mess. At work one day, I asked the guard who looked after us why the Al-Qaeda women could have all that when I couldn't even have a hairband. Normally, she was a cool person, but my question came at the wrong time and she gave me a lesson about drug-dealers and how I should be grateful for my life. And, of course, how the French people's money was feeding me right now. I wished I hadn't said anything and hoped she wouldn't file a complaint about me.

When she calmed down, she threw what seemed like thousands of envelopes onto my desk.

Great.

As I looked around me, a few women gave me a stupid smile. There was a crazy Chinese woman who always had a mad look in her eyes. She took her finger and ran it across her throat, while she licked her lips.

"Don't go to the showers today," Matilda said quietly. "They are angry now, but they will forget by tomorrow."

I didn't go.

The showers were a great place to go if we wanted to have a chat before bed. The only trouble was that some women liked to fight there or "sort out their problems". Sometimes, people would stare madly at my body when I was naked and soapy.

The guards let you in and then locked the door. They would come to pick you up when they thought you might be clean and take you back to your cell. Sometimes, it could be 40 minutes, sometimes 10, depending on the guard or their mood on that day, or whether they were enjoying the book they were reading, or how long they were on the phone.

They liked to turn off the water without warning. So we often had to swipe off the bubbles with a towel or try to wash them off in the sink, but that wasn't as effective as the soap would dry on our skin, leaving it really itchy. My skin wasn't just dry, it was extra dry, but for the time being, I could only dream about body lotion.

Nobody cared what was happening inside the locked showers. We could have killed each other in there; that was our own business. That's why it was very important to be on good terms with everyone, or there would be blood, slaps, spitting or razor attacks.

Sometimes, these fights happened at the library as well. We could go there for an hour at the weekend. Women mostly went to do their hair, chat and slag each other off, but sometimes, slaps would fly.

I was probably the only one who went to the library to exchange books and actually read them. I tried to pretend that I was not even there. We were locked in, unsupervised, for an hour; anything could happen in that time...

"Apparently, you read books from the library?" my psychologist said during one of our sessions.

"I've read all of them now."

"Really?"

"Well, you only have a few English ones. Once I'd read them, I started to read the French ones too."

"Can you read French?"

"No."

"So how do you read them?"

"I've borrowed a French dictionary; I am translating words like that."

"How?"

"Word by word."

"Ivana, you are very clever."

"No, I am just very depressed and desperate."

I wrote a letter to the prison manager to ask if I could please have my hairband and clips from my luggage. This was somewhere downstairs in the cellar, next to our workshop. My hair was getting so long now and getting in my way, especially at work.

The answer came back two weeks later. Apparently, I had to ask the guards, but as the prison management didn't feel this was very crucial, I was told not to bother prison workers about it.

"Why it is so hard to give a person two hair clips?" I cried to the psychologist. "Why do they want to make me feel absolutely worthless? We do have feelings too and basic human needs."

The psychologist only shook his head. "I can't give you an answer, Ivana," he replied, while I sniffed and wiped my tears on the massive blouse I was wearing. "Try to put this down as a lifetime experience. Don't let it get you down."

"Some women got a lighter in their cells. Meanwhile, I'm squinting because I've got nothing to tie my hair up with."

"Be patient."

"I have no more energy. I feel like this is the end of my life here."

"It is only one part of your life."

"It's is easy for you to say, nobody is shouting at you to be 'SILENT' all the time."

He didn't say anything and just stared at me.

"How many kilos do you weigh now, Ivana?"

"I don't know, maybe 44."

"You must eat; you will have no energy for all this."

# 19

# Stormy Weather

That spring in Paris was very rainy and there were lots of storms and thunder that made the guard dogs at the front go mad. I felt like a captured princess, imprisoned in an old, cold, stinky castle. When the rain hit the windows, the glass shook like it was going to smash. When there was lightning, shadows in my cell turned into scary monsters, and when the thunder hit, the window frames couldn't protect us from the cold or the noise.

I was scared and I wasn't the only one. Most of us sat on our beds and stared out of the window. It was like the lightning didn't just light up our cells, it even lit up our souls.

I wrapped myself in the blanket, closed my eyes and tried to dream about something nice. About warm coffee from Starbucks, a blueberry muffin, the gentle rain in London, where I would feel happy, safe and good behind the windows. On cold, wet evenings there, I would watch *Friends* or *Sex and the City*, eating lots of vanilla ice cream and flipping through the latest issues of magazines. How times had changed.

During the storms, I would cry and think about all those who were outside, living their lives without me, and I'd think about everything that I'd left. I knew I wouldn't just be able to step back into their lives after this madness, this crazy place.

It was around this time that a new woman came to the prison and had the cell right next to Marie's. She was Spanish and had long hair down to her waist. She didn't speak to anyone, but every night, at around 1a.m., she would take off her clothes, dance around and sing all kinds of ritual songs. She sang so loud, you simply couldn't miss her. It was always the same. She'd start by crying out, "Mr Robert, help me, I am dying!!"

Mr Robert was the prison manager. who was probably having a lovely sleep somewhere in his beautiful Parisian apartment with high ceilings. He definitely didn't care about this crazy woman who was keeping us awake.

After half an hour or so, she would stop for an hour and then carry on again until around 3a.m. By 4a.m., the dogs would start to go crazy, and I would sit on my bed and rock myself back and forth, crying and praying. I would pray to be strong and not give up, pray so that my life would not end in here, pray that I wouldn't go mad. Please morning, come quickly, please...

The problem was the Spanish women sang naked, and the guards weren't allowed to enter her cell if she had no clothes on. They could only talk to her from behind the door, and that just provoked her and made things worse. After six of those nights, everyone was so tired that we stopped talking to each other at work. Nobody spoke a word.

Marie was feeling very depressed at the time, and Matilda was waiting for the Spanish woman to show up for work, so that she could explain to her that this was a "decent prison".

I laughed when she said that. What kind of combination of words is that? "Decent prison."

On the seventh and eighth night, it was the same.

"Do something about her or I will kill her myself, and then you will finally have a reason to hold me here!" I said to the psychologist.

He nodded his head and told me to eat more.

"Don't worry about my eating habits. Make sure that we can sleep. Crazy people should go to the mad house."

A few days later, the woman disappeared.

Even after she'd gone, the storms and the dogs kept me awake. I was getting four hours sleep, at most; I couldn't rest and my body was in pain. We didn't chat much in those days. Even in my normal life, I find spring is quite a melancholic time, as my body is exhausted after the winter. Here in prison, you couldn't get excited about the prospect of having a picnic in Hyde Park or enjoying a coffee outside, somewhere nice. There was nothing to look forward to.

They brought another Spanish woman in and she also started some kind of trouble. God knows what her problem was. Even in work, she would start fights and throw envelopes at the guards and supervisor. As a punishment, they took the radio away from our workshop. The days seemed much longer without songs. I missed humming along to the tunes.

As we were escorted back to our cells for lunch one day, Matilda turned around to the guard and said, "Madam, something smells here."

"The whole prison smells, haven't you noticed? I clean my cell every day and it still stinks just like a cellar," I joked.

"But this is a different smell," she complained.

She was right. There was a terrible stench that smelled of both burning material and urine, mixed together.

We all stared at the guard and Matilda cried out, "Something is on fire!"

We were told to stop talking and the guard said she would take us all back to the workshop straight away.

Later on, we found out that the Spanish lady had managed to set fire to her own bed. She was so troublesome, they didn't let her out of her cell, but she managed to wreak havoc in there. Some of the women were really mad; they didn't belong in prison, but in a mental hospital.

If the fire had spread, it would quickly have become a massive problem. None of the doors or gates were easy to open. It always took ages to get them open with the massive keys the guards carried around, so there was no way we could get out in a hurry. I was concerned and asked our guard at work if the building was safe from the fire. She joked that I was skinny enough to slip through the bars on the windows, and I laughed to be polite, but the truth was there were no fire exits in this old castle-turned-prison.

# 20

## Getting By

During the last spring storms, I kept having a silly dream, over and over again.

Frenchy came to visit me, and couldn't take his eyes off my bad skin and greasy hair. He gave me a plastic bag.

"I was just passing by and stopped to find out if you are really here, so that I can see you with my own eyes and tell everyone back in London. Of course, I've brought you some clothes, as it must be terrible to wear prison gear all the time."

I'm not sure why I'd started to think about Frenchy; maybe because of all the fashion shows I watched on television, as there was nothing else to watch, and even that "nothing" was all in French. There were no movies or TV series, just news or documentaries about politicians, and I didn't care about politics. So if there was a little bit of fashion on TV, I watched it and enjoyed drinking in all the different aspects of my old life – lovely materials, fabrics, cuts and models, as well as the photographers, getting the best pictures from all angles. Tears would pour down my face. Even when I was psychologically messed up, watching this made me happy again for a few minutes.

Maybe that's why I had those silly dreams, because in prison, I had to walk around dressed like a homeless person in charity clothes. The only clothes of my own were some underwear that I had in Buenos Aires and one pair of jeans.

The rest of the clothes from my luggage were useless really. Bikinis, high heels, mini-skirts and cocktail dresses are of no use in prison.

We washed all the clothes we had by hand with soap and had to find some way of drying them in our cells. Matilda once asked for a dressing gown and the charity found one for her – a big, fluffy, red one. So when she decided to wash it, the three of us helped her to squeeze water out of it in the showers, giggling and messing about as we finished the job. It was a happy memory.

Our favourite guard, Madam Sabine, was always kind and let us swap stuff, like coffee, chocolate, sugar and magazines, between ourselves, even though it was forbidden. Lesley and I always swapped our magazines, although this was technically illegal! Everyone was always short of something, so there was a swapping system between friends. I was often short of whatever I needed, earned hardly anything, and had to pay off the drug debt. I also had a very expensive TV in my cell – not even five-star hotels charged as much – but if you don't want to go crazy in your cell, you really do need a TV.

The swapping process was simple. Once every fortnight, you got a piece of paper and wrote down what you needed – coffee, sweets, soap, face cream, shower gels, or maybe some extra food. Then, a couple of days later, Madam Sabine would open all our doors to take us to work, or the showers, and leave them open for a couple of minutes before locking them again. This gave us time to swap our stuff.

If she wasn't in work, we would hide stuff in our bras or pants instead. Trust me, if you get desperate, you will find a way to swap that extra bit off coffee for a tiny bit of hand cream.

Everyone who worked stuffing envelopes had very dry hands, with paper cuts and peeling skin. My skin would absorb a little bit of cream very quickly and scream for more. I didn't really have body lotion for months. My ankles were covered in bloody scratches because my skin was so itchy. Matilda swapped her face cream with my coffee. The only problem was that my skin didn't like it and I went all red and spotty!

Sometimes, we were forced to be creative with our swaps, especially during the weekends. Matilda came up with a special system, which used string and a plastic bag. Of course, it was a massive problem if anything fell out of the bag, and it only worked in a few places in the building. I remember someone once trying to transport eggs, but they made a huge noise when they hit the floor. If the guards had found them, the whole floor would have been in trouble. Luckily, it was now summer, so most French people were on the French Riviera, and those left at work didn't bother too much about anything, so nobody noticed.

Some of the guards were kind enough to bring items to swap from one cell to another if you asked nicely and behaved well. They were human, after all, and I even felt sorry for some of them. Not for all of them, however, as there were guards that treated prisoners like animals, just because they could.

It was easy to forget that we were all the same for some of the guards. In their eyes, I was not Ivana, the girl used by drug-dealers, but a dealer who didn't deserve normal treatment. Some of them saw us as trash and would take their bad moods and family problems out on us.

The most popular word was "SILENCE!", which I heard non-stop, as it was the answer to nearly every question. I sometimes imagined they must have lined up all their recruits against a wall and seen who could shout it out the loudest.

# 21

## *Missing John*

The weather was lovely at the end of April and beginning of May. I stood next to my cell window, looking at the city of Paris and breathing in the fresh air. I would close my eyes and imagine the fresh cut grass in my grandparents' garden. Sometimes, I even felt I could see my grandparents waving at me.

It was great to go out in the garden. I remember one of those afternoons, when I sat with Matilda on the grass, dreaming about ice cream and a good Frappuccino. I imagined we were at Hyde Park, in a cool, peaceful spot…

As we sat there, chatting about men, a few other women joined us. It began to look like a kind of girl scout club, as we were all talking about our experiences with men.

"Why do you keep talking about John?" Matilda asked. "John messed up your head. Your real love was a Frenchman."

"My Frenchman was always thinking about work, rather than me, and he got another girlfriend pretty quickly!"

"And by now, John is sleeping with a new model, trust me. I know 'our men', those who like white women. For men like him, it doesn't matter which girl, only if she is white."

"What? That's crazy. Why do you assume that?"

"John made you happy with his big, black dick."

"Matilda, be quiet," I giggled.

"That was his job, you know. He probably knows the people that got you in here."

"Matilda, you are so sharp."

"Life teaches me to be. People only do things that benefit them, and men twice as much!!"

"I am very sorry I never told John I loved him."

"You are a bloody idiot."

I could feel the tears pricking my eyes, so Matilda changed tack to cheer me up. "Stop this man talk. Just focus on getting out of here and your career, when you are released. Both John and your Frenchy should apologise to you!"

Lesley sat next to us. She was in good mood, as she had a fresh pack of cigarettes, and so she could smoke like a normal person, rather than try to get the most out of a half-centimetre stub.

"When I get back home, I will smoke from morning to night." I knew she would as well.

"Do you miss home?" I asked.

"I miss everything English."

"Me too," I nodded.

"It looks that I might be leaving at the end of the month. My daughter went to the embassy, she is on it."

I swallowed hard. My embassy didn't care.

"My daughter is ashamed of me. She doesn't want anything to do with me anymore. She's had enough," said Lesley.

"She will be OK," Matilda said. "She's only got one mum"

Lesley lit up another cigarette, took a deep breath and shook her head.

"You don't know her. She is pig-headed. She will be a good daughter when I am about to die, but until then, I don't exist.

"Why?" I asked.

"Because we live so differently: me, like a teenager, her, like a middle-aged woman going through the menopause." We all laughed. "I am always having man trouble and swapping boyfriends, while she lives with one man who she met at high school. The most fun they have is watching *Britain's Got Talent.*"

"Simon Cowell," I giggled. "Maybe he's her secret love?"

"If she did have someone like him, I would have gone home a long time ago."

"Don't carry drugs in your pockets," said Matilda, starting a now-familiar lecture. "If you carry cocaine like sweets then your own child will have to rescue you."

Lesley didn't smile, she just carried on smoking. I could see she was very upset.

Maybe here in the prison, she could reflect on her life for the first time in years. It was perhaps the first time in her life that she had a chance to think, without anyone disturbing her, and analyse the last few years, and realise she could live better.

I tried to support her with a quiet smile, as I understood her self-doubt. I also faced these dark thoughts when I couldn't sleep on my hard bed – doubts about whether I'd lived my life in the right way, and doubts about the people around me. At these times, I would analyse my memories, wondering where it all went wrong.

There were a few women sitting next to us, some of them with cigarettes, some just like Lesley. I realised, as they shared their stories, that they were all wives, lovers, mothers and daughters, who each had an "outside" family. Some started to share their stories, passing round tiny photos of their families. Their lives had been simple, but they had all known love. As I listened to their stories, I had tears in my eyes. All of them had someone waiting for them on the outside.

I didn't.

John had forgotten about me.

"Your black man has left you," Matilda told me. "He loves successful white women, but now you're in prison, with no success, he doesn't love you…"

That night, I couldn't sleep. I had all kinds of thoughts in my head. I desperately needed a hug and for someone to tell me it was only a bad dream. Instead, I just hugged a pillow in my arms and tried to fall asleep. In the end, I drifted into an uneasy sleep.

# 22

## Anorexia

My favourite prison guard came to my cell one Saturday afternoon. I was sitting on my bed, watching a fly that was trying to get out of the window. But I didn't want to let it out just yet, as I didn't want to be alone. I had reached a new low.

"I need to speak to you."

"Yes, madam." I stood up, a little worried, as this had never happened before.

"Some people are worried about you."

"I don't understand."

"Well, they are worried."

"Why? I am OK."

She took out a bunch of keys from behind her belt and shook them. It was a nasty noise. Even the fly was scared and started buzzing.

"Can you hear that noise?" she said, pointing to the keys.

I nodded.

"That's just like the noise your bones are making."

"What are you trying to say, madam?"

"Only that you are getting skinnier and skinnier."

"I am OK."

"No one in here is OK, you know that."

"I feel OK."

"You don't look good, or even OK."

"Of course not. I don't wear any make-up, have any good face cream or shampoo, and my hands are like an old woman's."

"Have you eaten anything today?"

"No, I didn't like lunch."

"And breakfast?"

"You mean that three-day-old bread roll and a tiny blob of butter?"

"Yes, that is what I mean."

"I lost my appetite."

"That's not good. You don't eat anything to keep you going during the day, and I know you do exercises here at night."

"I've been this way for most of my life."

"People are saying that you have anorexia."

"This is not anorexia. I don't starve myself. When I am hungry, I eat."

"You sure?"

"I miss my family and my boyfriend. Being locked up is a struggle."

"Other women eat here."

"Don't worry about me, really."

"OK, but try to eat more, please."

When she left, I got up and opened the window to let the fly out.

There you go.

# 23

# *Bullies*

After that, a few women commented on my body in the shower. Apparently, I was only skin and bone. Some of them even said that I was trying to starve myself to death in prison.

I kept quiet, even though I wanted to tell them to mind their own business or have a good look at their own fat bodies. I thought I was a healthier weight than some of them, but there was no point explaining this. Some of them really tried to provoke me, but I did my best to bite my tongue. I knew they were just waiting for my reaction.

When they didn't get one, they tried a to piss me off in other ways – with food.

Our prison didn't have a dining room, so everybody ate in their own cells. For breakfast, we got an old bread roll, cheap from a bakery that couldn't sell it when it was fresh, the tiniest piece of butter. We were also given lukewarm water, which wasn't hot enough, with sachets of something that smelled like coffee, but was probably chicory – something that my old grandma used to make me when I was a little girl.

As a snack, we would normally get an apple or orange. Lunch and dinner were classics, like pasta, vegetables, and sometimes meat. Other prisoners would bring our food to our cells with the guards. It was a hard work, as there were lots of cells on four floors and everyone needed a meal.

One of the women who had a "problem" with me in the showers then came to serve me lunch and deliberately tripped, throwing my food all over the floor.

"Sorry," she laughed, deliberately treading on the food to make it worse.

Sometimes, she didn't even bother to pretend to slip, but simply chucked the meat and potatoes on the floor, saying that I wouldn't eat it anyway.

It made me so angry, not because I wanted the food, but because it was so perverse, and a reminder that I didn't belong there. I hadn't done anything wrong, and my life was so different to the lives of such crazy scumbags.

I was also angry that the guards didn't do anything about it. They didn't care. Some of them thought we were all the same, and when food was thrown on the floor, it was just business between prisoners.

The mean women delivering the food also found out who was saving their cigarettes for a rainy day and started stealing them. When people realised this, there was a big fight in the library. I hid behind some bookshelves and prayed no one would notice me, as it was the last thing I needed. Most of these women were mothers, and I wondered why they hadn't had their children taken away from them.

During the summertime, these nasty women had another cruel trick. They would bring my lunch early, before I got back from the workshop, open my windows and leave it uncovered. So when I got back, my room was full of pigeons and bird poo. And, of course, there was nothing to eat. If the food was on the floor, I could pick something up, as I kept it very clean. I bleached and mopped it every day because I didn't have anything else to do.

When those bullies still didn't get a reaction from me, they would make something up to tell my workshop boss. One day, my boss came into my cell before work and told me that I had to take all my pictures off the walls as a punishment.

I had no idea what she had been told; it must have been something terrible, as I made sure I was well behaved to all the staff (because even a little problem could cost me some extra months in that madhouse).

"What?" I said, shocked by her order.

"Everything on the walls has to be taken down!"

"But why, madam?"

"As punishment"

"What kind of punishment?"

"You know very well, so hurry up with it or you will be late for work!"

She looked at me in a way that told me there was no point in arguing, so I started to take my pictures off the walls.

"Oh my God."

I couldn't stare at the dirty, nasty walls every day. Those pictures were like my little world. I had most of the fashion icons next to my mirror, and pictures of fashion designers, like Jacobs, Lagerfeld, Cavalli, which I found in Lesley's magazines, on my wall. Next to my bed, I had a picture of 50 Cent, so he was the first thing I saw in the morning. I didn't want to take him off, but I had no choice.

That morning, I lost it, stamping my legs, pulling my hair out and shouting all the English, Slovak and French swear words I knew. Tears were pouring down my face as I screamed at the boss and those bullies.

Then I ran out of words. I was desperate. Where was John to protect me? The bitches had finally got me.

# 24

# My Secret Admirer

*"I am terrifically meant to be to have left without having opened you my heart, but this became penible and dificult for me to know you, hello my sweetheart Ivka."*

That was how the letter began. I found it in my letterbox and it was written in very bad English. It made no sense to me.

*"In such misery and to be able to make nothing. I hope on the contrary no to have made a lot ot errors dorthographe and of expression because it is about a translation performed via a dictionary!!"*

The letter was full of support, understanding and love. It wasn't from John; his English is perfect and he never talked about that kind of stuff. Also, most people don't know that Ivka is short for Ivana in Slovakian. It had been typed on a computer and there was no signature or return address.

I quickly checked out the envelope. It had been sent from Paris two days ago. Who the hell could it be? None of my French friends knew where I was.

I read the letter few more times. Hmmmm.

It could have been a bad joke by one of the prisoners, but where the hell would they have got access to a computer?

Only the Al-Qaeda girls had computers, but they didn't even know who I was. Then I wondered if it was someone working in the prison, but no one would risk anything like that. I came up with a third theory later in the evening, and the more I thought about it, the more likely it seemed.

That cute French policeman, who had been nice to me when I was arrested, would have access to all the information. And he was from Paris.

It sounded ridiculous, but it couldn't be anyone else.

How romantic and how bloody crazy?

That letter definitely changed my mood, even though I realised I would have to be careful. It could be a trap; a gentle, romantic trap. I would wait and see what happened.

A few days later, another letter came. This one started by saying:

> "My life without you is only empty in nonexistence…"

It was very sweet. Besides lots of lovely compliments, the person asked me to be discreet and then, at the end of the letter, urged me to eat.

I didn't know what to think. I wanted to be grown up and think everything through properly, but I was giggling just like a teenager instead and dancing around my cell with the letters.

I don't know if you can understand what it was like, but imagine being totally isolated, surrounded by foreign people, and half of them are mad and out to get you. A letter like this wakes up all those sleeping endorphins. I felt just like a teenager with a secret I couldn't even tell my best friend. I didn't say anything, not even to Matilda, Marie or Lesley, who was now back home in England. I enjoyed this anonymous correspondence because it was a ray of sunshine in my depressing life.

Every time I came back to the cell, my eyes went straight to my letterbox. It was mostly empty, but I was so happy when there was something in there. It was like checking your Facebook inbox.

When the third letter arrived, I opened it so fast. That letter started by saying:

> *"Intends more for me only to be able to belong to you one day… i give you my heart, my body and my sex. All that for you and alone you!"*

Oh my God! This letter was more intimate than the previous two. It was very personal. I didn't know why but it made me cry. I didn't know if that was because I was so sad or very happy. I still thought the author was the black policeman, but I couldn't remember his face very clearly.

Anyway, it didn't matter who the letters were from; they were a balsam for my soul. Never mind if it was pathetic, I didn't care, not even when the English was very bad. There were parts I couldn't understand properly, like:

> *"I want you to be my pillar, my soul mate, the one whom i can count. I want to form only single blog with me. I want the fruit of love to be born of our union. I want to share my whole life with you and i am ready to leave everything and to live my passion with you, becouse it is you that i want to be… a day in your side valleys*

*better then one thiousand elsewhere. You are*
*what there is more precious and marvels in my*
*opinion. I want to concrete my dream which*
*is to have you as a companion until death*
*separetes us."*

I read this letter a million times. Do you remember I said I could not understand the man who tamed the mouse in *The Green Mile* and had turned my head away in disgust? Now I got it. He loved his mouse and that love stopped him from going crazy. Now I had love from these letters, from a policeman I didn't love. But I loved the letters with a strange kind of love.

If those letters had disappeared or someone had stolen them, I would have had a meltdown. They become both my love and my world.

# 25

# *The Phone Call*

All this time, while sitting behind bars, I was trying non-stop to get out as soon as possible. I was always writing to charities and anyone else who could possibly do anything about this mess. I was frustrated that lots of women on drug charges got out a lot faster than me. I was entitled to legal help, but my lawyer kept telling me the same things over and over again.

"You must be well behaved, pay as much as you can, and in six months, you will have a trial, and if that goes well, you can get out early."


My cousin, Danka, wrote frequently and helped me organise a few things. I didn't want to get my parents involved, as my dad was on health benefits and so had to live on my mum's wage. If they had known how much I had to pay, it would have made them sick with worry. As they couldn't help me, there was no point in telling them.

"You've got one disadvantage," my psychologist told me.

"And that is?"

"Modelling."

"I don't understand."

"Everyone thinks that you are some kind of celebrity, so they try to get more money out of you."

"Who do you mean by 'everyone'?"

"The decision makers."

"The judge and those people?"

"Yes. The judge and those people."

"But I am not a celebrity!"

"They don't know that."

"Why don't you tell them?"

"I can only try to make the point in your review."

"So it would be much easier for me if I was a shop assistant."

"With your behaviour, yes."

"Oh my God, what kind of world is this?"

"Do you need any pills?"

"No, please stop asking about pills."

"Why don't you try to learn French? That would be something positive to put in your review."

I took lessons once a week after work, but sometimes, I was far too tired and had a headache, so it was difficult to focus. It seemed quite a difficult language to learn.

The teacher was a typical Frenchwoman, with a ring on every finger.

At the beginning of the lesson, she smiled and said, "I speak English quite well but for your own good, I will be communicating only in French with you."

Half asleep, everyone nodded.

"She can speak what she wants, even Swahili, but I just do not have the energy to listen to her," Matilda joked. Somehow, we made it through those lessons.

By prison rules, I was only allowed one phone call a month. Of course, I had to submit all the details of who I wanted to call in writing and then wait for a reply. Sometimes, I waited so long, I forgot all about it.

One day, when the French teacher was explaining something about grammar, the door opened and guards came in to pick me up.

"Ivancakova, you can go and make a call."

"What?" I was confused; I wasn't ready to speak to my parents in just a few seconds.

Mum answered the phone after one ring. Her voice was so kind and gentle.

"Mummy?" I managed.

"Ivka!" she shouted, and I could see her in front of my eyes.

I was trying my best not to cry, but it was impossible. Mum started to cry and I could hear Daddy crying too.

"Ivka, is it really her?" he was asking. His voice was shaking. It is terrible to hear your own daddy cry. He was a very strict, honest, hard man and I had never heard him like this before.

"How are you, Ivka?" Mum asked.

"Good, Mum it's OK," I answered, as tears poured down my cheeks and onto the phone. Mum was also crying, and then the guards came to tell me to finish the call after just a few minutes. I just managed to say, "I love you, Mum," before I was made to put the phone down.

I felt terrible.

They brought me back to the French lesson, but I wasn't listening to what the teacher was talking about, only the rain that was knocking against the windows, reminding me of London.

And I noticed the teacher's coffee mug. It was red with the Nescafe logo on it. Just like my mum's.

# 26

## Michael Jackson

Another woman arrived. The gossip around prison was that she had chopped her husband's head off while he read the newspapers. The police only found his body and she refused to tell anyone where the head was.

She looked quite young and was always talking to herself. I saw her in the garden by chance, while I was waiting in a queue. I was so scared of her but couldn't pinpoint why. I could feel bad energy from her and kept thinking that she would pull out a knife from somewhere and hurt me.

On 25th June, she shouted at me in French, and it must have been nasty as Marie didn't want to translate it. She just said I must look like the lover of this woman's husband. Well, that was just great.

They came to wake us a little bit later than usual the next day. Breakfast was late and the coffee cold. I wondered whether they had thrown a staff party or were just feeling lazy. Something was up.

Even when they came to pick us up an hour later for work, my boss was quiet and held a little radio in her hands.

When we got to the workshop, I decided to find out what was going on.

"Marie," I whispered across the table, "today is payday; why does everyone look like they are at a funeral?"

"You didn't hear?"

"No, what?"

"Michael Jackson has died."

"Oh God."

"Television is full of it."

"I didn't switch on my television."

"That's why everybody looks so weird."

"I've got tickets for his concert in London."

"Well, they are good for nothing now."

"They are good for nothing anyway, as I'm stuck in here all summer."

The next day was John's birthday.

I hadn't heard a word from him in five months and I wanted to sleep all day.

I covered my head with my blanket and imagined John waking up somewhere in London, answering his phone, getting all his birthday wishes, and maybe cuddling some girl who had stayed over the night. Maybe he would have a big party, and after a few drinks, someone would ask about me. "Hey John, what happened to that Ivana girl? You know, that Slovak model you went out with last autumn?"

He would just wave his hand or maybe reply, "Ivana? I don't remember anyone called that."

And all of them would start to laugh.

"Happy birthday, John," I whispered into the pillow, with my eyes full of tears. *Do you think about me, sometimes? Why don't you write? I know the London lifestyle is very busy, but is there really no time for you to write? Do you miss me? Do you love me? Did you ever love me anyway?*

On Saturday 27th June, I found the book *Men Are from Mars, Women Are from Venus* in the library. It was an English copy as well and I hoped it might help me to understand why John didn't write.

# 27

# The Doctor

There was only one person in the whole prison that I really didn't like – the gynaecologist. He was an amateur doctor, amateur psychologist and an amateur human being.

I guess the prison management didn't mind giving such a sensitive job to this arrogant, unpleasant monster. He wore a dark-green doctor's overall and hated everything that was English. He apparently had a soft spot for black women, although that was just gossip. They told me he was a pervert.

"Why don't you girls write and complain about him?" I asked Matilda one day, when she was talking about him in the garden. Apparently, he had been checking her out in an unprofessional way.

"Because I would end up in the bin. It is our word against his, sweetheart, and we are criminals, while he is Mr Doctor."

"What if he hurts someone, someday? You know what I mean…"

"I do," Matilda nodded.

"Do we have to take all this shit because we are prisoners? Don't we have any rights?"

Matilda looked at me and laughed. "You've got the right to keep quiet and to keep on moving, and that's two rights. Is that not enough for you?"

I only went to see him because I needed the contraceptive implant in my arm taken out as it had expired. He told me off for speaking English and acted like he didn't understand what I was talking about, squeezing the area where the implant was.

"If you are a doctor, you would know that squeezing an area where an implant is placed is not a good idea."

"Am I the doctor or are you?"

"I have been informed by a doctor."

"English doctors will do anything for money."

"They do anything to make sure that their patients are OK."

"An implant is not healthy. I don't believe in contraception."

"I didn't ask you for your opinion. I am asking you if you can take it out and replace it."

"No."

"No?"

"No."

"Can I ask why?"

"You aren't going to have sex in here."

"I know, but the hormones help me with my skin problems."

"Ask the guards to get you some good face cream."

"It also helps with depression."

"You are never going to be happy here."

"What kind of person are you?"

"Is that all you wanted? Come here, while I do some check-ups."

I don't think so. I slammed the door; I didn't even try to be polite.

A few weeks later, one of the Brazilian girls showed me an implant that had been put in while she was in prison. Unbelievable!

And while I'm talking about sex, we all missed it, of course. You could often hear women shouting late into the night, "I need a f**k! Give me a man, I need to orgasm!"

You missed the cuddles, sweet talk, and all those intimate moments too. Lots of people have got a different idea about a women's prison. People think they are full of lesbians. Well, I don't think so. I didn't see any of that. Of course, it was lonely, and so you made friends with who you could. I don't think I would have become friends with people like Matilda if we'd met outside of prison. I don't mean to be rude in any way, it's just that our lives outside would be completely different, and we probably wouldn't have anything to talk about.

During the summer, when we had our windows wide open, we could see straight into the gym used by the male prison workers – security, guards, managers, and God knows who else. So during the weekends, when we didn't get checked that often, we 'd sit next to the windows and watch them. We even laughed on the days when we had a good guard and commented on what we saw. But, as always, the Spanish ladies ruined all the fun by shouting out stupid things.

Most of the prisoners were Spanish, Italian and African, but the work instructions were given in French, so most of us made up our own version of these instructions.

Even though we didn't understand each other, there was one word that all of us knew – "chupa-chups"! It was a made-up word that meant there was a good-looking man around. It could be a new guard or policeman bringing in or escorting prisoners, or a visitor, although we didn't have many of those.

Matilda was once told off for not wearing her work uniform. While reaching for it, she spotted the male guards' morning routine and shouted, "Madam, there is a lot of chupa-chups out there!"

To our surprise, the boss started to laugh and was even the first one to pile outside the window to stare at the men

We could choose one sports activity. Matilda told me at the beginning, when she first gave me some hand cream, that women don't do any exercise, they bloody fight.

Spring came and every woman seemed to be working out. The coach was a very handsome Frenchman, and it was such fun to watch all the women try to get his attention.

"I'd do a different kind of exercise with him…" said Matilda.

We all laughed, as all of us were missing a man. All of us.

Some of the women had someone waiting for them outside, some of them were hoping, and some of us were slowly losing that hope, but didn't want to let it go just yet.

I had my memories of John.

And the letters sent by someone from Paris who loved me in some strange kind of way.

I didn't stop believing in love. I would not have survived the hell of prison without it.

# 28

## The Gipsy Girl

Most of the prison personnel went on leave during the summer holidays. France is very strange in that way. Everything stops in the summer and so nobody was where they were supposed to be. They were either stuck in a traffic jam or enjoying a holiday in the south of France. Paris was full of tourists and the people who worked in businesses connected to tourism.

So there was no psychologist, social worker or assistant social worker in prison at that time. There wasn't even a judge; all of them were on holiday. It was much hotter than usual and nobody wanted to work. We had been forgotten about.

I was hoping that the summer would give me an energy boost, and the sun would fill me with hope and optimism. But it had the opposite effect. When I looked out of the window, my head was full of London streets, coffee shops, fun and vanilla ice cream.

To make matters worse, my friends weren't as chatty as usual. Even Matilda didn't want to talk. Marie hadn't been feeling well over the last few days and was clearly taking more pills. Her sister's clothes parcel hadn't arrived and she thought someone in prison had stolen it. Marie took this very personally, which was not surprising because of her psychological problems, so the psychologist gave her more tablets.

When the pills didn't help much, she decided to change her work to cleaning jobs to get more exercise. So we only saw her in the showers, at the weekend in the garden, or when she changed the bins in the workshop. She always waved to us with a smile on her face, and it did look like the cleaning job was helping, as she looked better by the end of the summer.

I killed time by watering the tomato plants I had planted in yoghurt pots. I was also trying to look after my itchy skin with all the creams that I could collect. I was so fed up. I thought I would die in prison by being bored to death. During the evenings, I didn't even bother looking outside anymore. Seeing Paris lit up only made me feel even worse, and in a French prison, it's so easy to get depressed… about everything.

\* \* \*

One Saturday morning, I didn't go into the garden as usual, and instead slept in and then cleaned my cell.

Matilda could see I had my window open and shouted, "You can clean later on, come outside now!"

So I put my flag out and waited to be picked up by a guard.

"Did you see her?" Matilda asked me, as soon as I arrived.

"Who?"

"The new one that came yesterday."

She pointed out a woman who was sitting on the bench, staring at the floor. She looked like a young gipsy woman.

"What's up with her?"

"Apparently, she killed two friends because they were gossiping about her."

"What?" I replied. I didn't understand.

"They were sitting in a coffee shop, and she was waiting for them on a tiny street and finished them off."

"That's strange."

"She told the police that they were slagging her off too much at the coffee shop."

"Was she there?"

"No."

"So, how did she know then?"

Matilda looked at me. "The guards are saying she is a witch." As she said the word "witch", the gipsy girl, who couldn't possibly hear us, lifted her head up and looked straight at us.

"Ohh my God, she is looking over here," Matilda gasped, panicking like a wild animal.

"Sweetie, please. You don't believe in this kind of rubbish, do you?"

That gipsy girl didn't make any friends and didn't speak to anyone. Later on, we heard that she had read a few women's palms and told them things about their past that she couldn't have known. Matilda decided to have her palm read and came back crying. The gipsy had told her that lots of people were just using her. She had bought houses, cars and paid the school fees for her whole family, who didn't even want to know her now.

I realised there could be some truth in that. She had been here for 15 months now and not received a single letter.

"Can you read for me too?" I asked her once at the library.

She spat three times on my hand – disgusting – and told me my Slovak friend was having a wedding this week, which was true, Anicka was getting married. I got a bit scared at that point, so I moved my hand a little bit but she held onto it tight. She then told me that I was a good person, but I should be careful of—

I didn't find out who or what that was because someone suddenly shouted. It was Marie, who screamed as loudly I had done when I'd found a family of dead rats in the garden.

Marie was dashing towards us, looking mad, but the gipsy girl touched her own sleeve and smiled at her. "These are your clothes, aren't they?"

A shiver ran down my spine when Marie nodded.

I held her by the wrist so that she couldn't fight. I could see the fire in her eyes.

# 29

# *Autumn Blues*

I was sitting in the second biggest prison in France. It had two parts – the biggest one was for men, and the smallest for women. They finished building it in 1898, which was probably why it was so stinky and cold during the long autumn days. There were many corners where the sun couldn't reach all the year round. Earlier that autumn, we had problems with the hot water and so could only have ice cold showers. As a result, most of the women got sick. The gipsy girl, who everyone took for a witch, said that she could feel death everywhere. A lot of had people died there, and not through natural causes.

Later on, when I was home, I looked up the history of the prison and they mentioned that Louis Renault, the automobile founder, worked for the Nazis there in 1944 and died in there as well. During the Normandy landings, the Germans killed all of the prisoners who were being kept there. Maybe that is why it had such bad energy. But then again, which prison has good energy?

By the time autumn came along, I was so desperate. My face was grey, lifeless and full of spots, as stress, desperation, cold showers and non-stop crying had made their mark on my skin.

My hair had no shape and the ends were dry and broken. I was losing so much hair, I ended up with a bunch in my hands if I ran my fingers through it. My eyes were red through both a lack of sleep and fresh air, and they had now lost their sparkle.

My hands looked like those of an old lady, dry and scratched. My nails were as soft as paper and full of white spots, generally a sign that your body is missing something. I didn't feel good, and when the first big cold spell arrived and our heating wasn't on, I got a sore back. Matilda had to massage my back every evening in the shower, and a Brazilian lady gave us some special healing lotion that burned my whole back. It did help, however, and I finally got some sleep. I woke up all stiff and in even more pain than the day before. After that, the cold moved to my head and I got a migraine, runny nose, and didn't have the energy to go to work. Instead, I had to spend a few days sitting in bed, wrapped up in a blanket with three pairs of socks on.

There was only enough hot water in my thermos bottle for tea until around 10a.m.; after that, I could only drink cold water from the sink, which gave me a sore throat.

It was a classic virus; millions of people all over the world got it. But they were able to lie in their own bed, while someone made them tea and brought fruit and food to their bedside. To recover, you have to rest, sleep a lot, sweat a lot and read, but I didn't have the energy to get better and wished that John was looking after me. I didn't have a reason to get better, and just lay listlessly or sat and watched television, wiping my red, sore nose. I stopped caring at this point.

The psychologist told me I was letting myself go, and he didn't like it, but his speech didn't interest me anymore, so I left the session early.

Even the thought of my favourite coffee and a blueberry muffin couldn't raise my spirits now, and I didn't have the energy to do my evening exercises anymore. I was simply lying in the bed coughing.

"Pull yourself together, girl," Matilda lectured me in the showers. "You must have happy thoughts, otherwise you will die of this cold. Work is busy now, we've got to stuff envelopes with a Christmas promotion, so come back and make some money. We miss you."

I sniffed and nodded, not feeling motivated about stuffing envelopes with bloody Christmas offers. I had nobody waiting for me. Nobody needed me.

I went back under my blanket, put on more socks and lay in the same position.

I also got constipated and sometimes couldn't go to the toilet for a whole week. I felt terrible, sitting for an hour on the toilet. The guards would check on me to see if I was still alive, so I would wave to them away from the toilet. I was quite embarrassed in the beginning but I stopped caring later on. I had to get used to a lot of stuff in that place, but I could never get used to the cold and spent hours shivering under the blanket. I would rub my knees together to make myself warmer and count the seconds until sunrise.

Around this time, I started to write a letter to John. I never intended to send it; I was only writing it for myself, so that I didn't go mad and could get all of the emotions out of my system that I was keeping inside my head. They were making me ill.

I wrote that I hated him for not writing to me and just carrying on with his own life. I also cursed him and said I didn't want to see him again. But even though I tried to be angry, my hand started to write how much I loved him and how much I missed his cuddles. I wrote a few letters and they all ended with the words: "John, why? Why?"

Sometimes, I wrote 10 or 15 pages and would lie exhausted on my hard pillow after I finished, before falling sleep and having absurd dreams.

# 30

## *Paris Fashion Week*

Paris Fashion Week was in October and I saw a few clips of it on television – interviews, shows and snapshots of bling life. The week is always accompanied by a lot of charity events, as fashion is for everyone, not just the "chosen" few. This motto is increasingly popular with fashion designers. They know what they're doing and think everything through very carefully. After all, the more people wear their clothes, the more money they make.

So fashion week came to our prison too.

Nathalie Cogno is a fashion designer who cares about making fashion inclusive. She often runs events; firstly, because she has a good heart and also, because these events are good publicity. Television, newspapers and magazines can all use her story to cover fashion week from a different angle.

The evening before I was asked to work on the prison fashion show, Matilda gave me a signal on the radiator to turn on my TV so that I could watch an hour-long interview with 50 Cent, with no dubbing, just French subtitles. This was something special for me!!!

The singer talked about his life and his ups and downs, which was interspersed with his songs. It was the quickest hour I had in prison. I remember one sentence he kept repeating: "You can only rely on yourself; if you start to rely on the people around you, things might not be done the way that you like."

I nodded to myself. Exactly. Don't expect anything from anyone; you can only trust yourself. If a helping hand does show up, it's a nice bonus, but don't expect it.

\* \* \*

Fashion Défilé, or a fashion show in prison, basically means that a designer brings some of the outfits from a collection to the prison, and the prisoners can put their own stamp on the final look of the outfit. They don't have many resources to change the outfits, just a few bows and sequins. Later on, a prisoner models the restyled outfit on the catwalk.

Everyone was quite sure they wanted me to take part in this, but I didn't want to.

I would have to give up a few work sessions and also my French lessons, which was a lot of money and points. No charity was going to help me with the money that I needed; I had to do it myself.

Just like 50 Cent said!

I also felt quite reluctant to work on a fashion show with women that had no idea about fashion because they spent most of their lives dealing in drugs.

\* \* \*

On Sunday morning, my favourite guard asked me why I was not taking part in the fashion show. Although she was not working on the day of the show, the guard said she would love to come and see me on the catwalk.

I shrugged my shoulders.

"You prefer to sit here and stare at the TV?" she asked.

I shrugged again.

"Ivana, there are women in the library, talking, laughing and spending time with professionals. They will forget that they are in prison for a few weeks."

"I don't know any of them."

"Is that the real reason?"

How could I tell her what was really going on inside me? How could I tell her that I'd always imagined my first catwalk in Paris would be very different? How could I write something like this down on my fashion CV?

"Madam, I don't feel like it."

"You? You should be teaching them."

I took a deep breath, and then she left.

I stayed all by myself within my four walls, and could hear music and giggling from somewhere inside the building.

I met Matilda in the garden that afternoon, wearing what clothes I could get from the prison or other prisoners, as I didn't had any warm clothes of my own to wear. Everything was a different size, shapeless and strange. The colours didn't match either, so I looked like a jester.

Claire, an English lady who had entered prison looking anorexic, had now put on some kilos after just a few months. A lovely lady, she helped me a lot, and not just by giving me clothes.

Some of the clothes were too big and in neon colours with strange prints, but I didn't care; I needed to be warm. I couldn't afford to get ill again. I might not be able to make it next time.

"I don't understand why they are forcing you to take part in that fashion show," Matilda said, shaking her head. "If you don't want to do it then don't do it."

"Maybe they're offended by a model saying no to them."

"Sweetie, only do what you want to do. You shouldn't care about what others think about it."

"I know."

"They will get paid for organising the show and buy their kids nice Christmas presents, while we're stuck here on hard mattresses with no money to buy family presents."

"You're right," I said, shivering at the thought of Christmas in my cold cell.

"You don't have to prove anything to anybody."

"Exactly."

"If you don't want to do it then forget about it."

I nodded.

"But, if I was in your shoes, I would be already teaching the rest of them how to walk on the catwalk."

In the end, my wall of disinterest, apathy and depression were broken down by Matilda's little lie.

\* \* \*

The next day, just before lunchtime, the guard came to pick me up. Apparently, the psychologist wanted to see me.

"Psychologist?" I was surprised. "Madam, if I remember correctly, my next session is next week."

"He wants to see you."

She took me to the floor where his office was, but we didn't walk in there.

Instead, the room we entered was full of prisoners that I didn't know, as well as a few people from "outside" (they looked too good to be from prison), the manager of the prison, Matilda and Marie.

"What's going on?" I asked.

The lovely people said something then the manager, with Marie translating. All the collection was ready now and they were showing me the outfits they would like me to wear. The clothes had to be fitted and they wanted me to come up with some kind of choreography.

"Ivana, do it," Marie whispered to me.

"Do it for us, it would be an experience."

So I had no choice. "I'll do it," I said.

"You made the right decision," Matilda replied, with a smile on her face.

"You will be not modelling in Paris for the next five years, so why not do it now?"

I had to laugh.

I spent that evening walking up and down in my cell, remembering some of the shows that I had done during my old life, before being imprisoned. It made me cry again.

The prison fashion show turned out to be quite nice in the end. All the girls' make-up was quite strong. Some complained about having too much on, but this was probably done for the media. I felt peaceful as I walked down the catwalk. It was good to see Matilda smiling. Marie had tears in her eyes and my favourite guard even made it to the show, despite not working that day. With most of the staff and prisoners moving to the rhythm of the music, it felt like a party.

"Watch out for the carpet in the corner of the catwalk," I whispered to the other "models". "The tape is not secure," I warned. "My shoes got stuck on it."

They nodded. Being a little bit shy, they listened carefully to everything I said. Some of them nervously held me by the elbow with their cold, wet hands until it was their time to go on. Every one of them was counting into the rhythm of the music, so they would get out on the catwalk on time.

When they came back, I told them to go and see the stylists and make-up artists, and change their outfits.

It was exciting, despite all the stress. There is sometimes a little bit of chaos backstage, but you can't see anything on the catwalk, as the models have to keep a professional face and have a strong, confident walk. I was proud of our prison models. To close the show, we all walked together and everybody clapped, while the DJ gave me the thumbs up. The party finished a little bit earlier than planned as women started to fight over the sweets – grown-ups and Italians.

Never mind. I was euphoric after the fashion show and happy in my own skin – I hadn't felt like that for months. There was a photographer from *Marie Claire* magazine called Nathalie, I think, who was really nice and caring. After taking me to one side, she asked the guards if she could take some pictures of me in different parts of the prison, for her use only. They said yes.

Even though I knew many pairs of eyes were watching me, I did love her taking my pictures. Nathalie gave me a copy of British *Vogue* and whispered that on one of the pages, I would find a contact. I nearly started to kiss the fat magazine. Tears were pouring down my face again, from happiness.

"Don't worry, you will be home soon," she said, and gave me a hug. "It's not over for you, you must see this as only an experience. You are a strong girl."

I gave her a hug back and nobody told me off, as there were a lot of press people around and the guards were trying to act like this was some sort of camp, rather than a real prison.

That night, my room was cold and there was food from the whole day on my table. After washing my make-up off, I put my flag out to go for a shower, and looked forward to reading the fashion bible when I got back.

The guard picked me up and on my way to the showers, I saw the manager walking to one of the cells with a packet of cigarettes in his hands.

Wow, someone is lucky, I thought.

When I returned to my clean, cold cell, my *Vogue* wasn't there, and nobody knew anything about it.

It had simply disappeared.

French assholes.

# 31

## Trial Date

I saw some coverage of our fashion show on television. Understandably, they blurred out the faces of the models, so their identities weren't clear. You could see the rest of our bodies, however. I have a very clear tattoo around my hips, which anyone who's worked with me or knows me from shoots would recognise. I just hoped these guys would not be interested in watching a prison fashion show. That would be embarrassing.

After the fashion show, the women started gossiping and whispering that I had been sleeping with the manager.

Hahahahaha!

All of them knew that it wasn't possible or even theoretically practical, but they had to get back at me after the fashion show because I got the most attention. Marie had warned me about it at the beginning.

"Really, I am sleeping with the manager? So why is my radiator not working then?" I replied, raising my eyebrows.

Marie started to giggle. "Well, because he comes over to keep you warm."

We both laughed like mad, but I did notice some of the nasty looks as well.

It was sad that the girls I had helped on the fashion show now started to hate me. They had flipped 180 degrees. Oh well, it was their problem.

It was bloody cold by November and when there was no hot water, it was all too much.

We had to go to the library so that we didn't freeze inside our cells. Lots of us packed into one small room, breathing over one another, which gave the illusion it was a warmer place.

As Matilda was looking pretty down, I wanted to cheer her up and give her some energy. So I took one of the letters along from my secret admirer. By this time, I had received three of them.

"I think it is from the policeman who was investigating my case when they arrested me," I said very quietly.

As soon as she started reading them, her eyes started to sparkle and I realised I had scored. She was keen to start her own investigation to discover who the author was. Knowing her, she would probably find him straight away and label us as a married couple.

"Oh girl, maybe God sent him for you."

"What are you on about?"

"God sent him as a replacement for the hell that you're living right now."

"Well, they are lovely letters."

"These are not just lovely letters, they are perfect love letters in bad English."

"I don't know him."

"But you said he is a policeman."

"I don't know him. I only saw him a few times."

"Oh, this is so romantic."

"It's just like from a movie, isn't it?"

Matilda nodded and then looked at me. "You should really give him a chance, you know, he is taking lots of risks for you!"

"Matilda, I love John."

"Oh, that one?"

"You think I am stupid?"

"Of course not. Love is stupid."

"Maybe God sent me to this prison, so that I could wake up and focus on things that are more important in life than modelling."

"And that is?"

"Family"

"Bullshit. You're made for modelling."

I was looking at her, trying to figure out if she was being sarcastic or not.

"After this experience, I won't even be made for casting," I said quietly. "The world of fashion is passé for me now, Matilda."

"Rubbish. Look at this from the other side – it's made you stronger and changed your values in life. You will have more to offer than the other stupid clothes hangers."

"So you think that models are stupid clothes hangers?"

"Everybody thinks that, sweetheart."

The prison radiators kept going on and off, as the one 100-year-old heating system wasn't working properly. So the prison manager had a plan B and changed all the windows in the whole building. Yes, in November. He decided we needed new windows that didn't let the cold in.

The logistics were difficult, as you couldn't be there while they were changing the windows in your cell. When they finished, you had to clean up the builders' mess, which wasn't easy without hot water.

"I have had enough of this prison," Matilda would complain. "I wish I could have a bath and stop worrying about running out of coffee."

I nodded. We were waiting in the library while they changed our windows. We both realised that Christmas was very soon, as there were lots of Christmas adverts all over TV. None of us would say out loud the words "Christ punch", "Christmas tree" or "family" because we were all feeling very gloomy about it.

By this time, I knew my trial would be just before Christmas. So if everything went well, I could possibly be home for the festive season. This was the only thing that could cheer me up, and as Matilda was going downhill, she didn't have any hope. It was not that she didn't want me to go, she just couldn't imagine being in prison without me.

* * *

As well as the windows, they changed our TVs for bigger models with English channels, but they didn't work yet, of course.

One thing that did work was the prison alarm, which woke me up every day for breakfast at 6a.m.

Boiled water was poured into the thermos bottle. After that, I was bored again, as there wasn't much work available in November, which was strange, considering the time of year. But I didn't want to worry about that because I felt poisoned by this cell now.

"Ivancakova," the guard said, after noisily opening the door to my cell. "The manager is waiting for you."

Wow, I wondered what it was. The thought crossed my mind that maybe he'd found my copy of *Vogue* or knew the reason for its disappearance. I was escorted to the manager's office, but it wasn't about my magazine, it was something much better!

The manager informed me that my trial would be on 19th November. I was delighted, as it meant they could soon be sending me home!

I was hopeful that they would let me off half of my sentence for good behaviour and hard work. My psychologist said the money I'd earned was much more than anyone here had ever paid and those prisoners had all been sent home much earlier as well.

"Just remember, you knew what you were doing," the social worker kept saying. "Don't give them any other version."

"OK, if you think so."

"I don't think, I know so," she said, making her views clear.

"The second you say that you didn't know about the drugs, you will be automatically booking yourself into a long stay in prison over the next few years."

"So nobody cares about the truth?"

"If they wanted to prove that you are innocent, they would have to look for witnesses, which would take a few years. Meanwhile, you will be here, slowly dying. No one puts much effort into three kilos of cocaine, there are much bigger sharks to catch."

"But still…"

"I do understand, but the people who helped to put you in prison vanished a long time ago. They are living their lives somewhere with completely different identities, and you are only one of many people they have used.

"So if I keep saying that I knew about the drugs, they will let me go home?"

"I don't know that for sure, but you've got a good chance. We rarely get a prisoner as good as you."

"Thanks."

"Don't thank me. If you believe in God then pray. If your judge has a bad night's sleep, all our luck could disappear."

I nodded in agreement; I had to believe that everything would go well and I'd be home for Christmas! Home. In Slovakia, with my mum, who now had health problems, thanks to me, and my father, who would still be by my side, even after all of this. I would spend Christmas with them in my old bedroom, where I could turn off the light whenever I wanted to.

# 32

# My Trial

The day of my trial finally came and I was up long before the nasty prison alarm went off. I don't know if I slept at all. If I did, it was only a nervous snooze – full of strange dreams that didn't make any sense, even though they were disturbingly similar to my reality at the time. I didn't touch breakfast and used all the water from my thermos bottle for a big coffee. Nervously, I sat in my chair drinking it, while waiting for the guards to take me to the trial room downstairs.

After a few months, I was wearing some of my own clothes again; the black pencil skirt I bought in Buenos Aries, with a white shirt and black cravat. This trial reminded me of everything I had been put through 10 months ago, and my stomach was churning. Once again, everyone's eyes were on me, everybody was staring, and some of the police officers made funny noises. I don't know how those guards even got their jobs; they were idiots.

I saw a few stressed-out women who looked in a terrible state in the hallway. They were probably waiting for their trial to begin after a few nasty nights in the holding cells. God knows what fate was in store for them. I saw professionals, like Matilda, who were pissed and trying to figure out who had grassed them up. The naïve ones, like myself, just felt lost and hopeless.

I wondered whether they had also met that cute policeman.

I hadn't got any letters in a long time now. Maybe he had lost his dictionary.

The main judge didn't even look at me. Studying the paperwork, he asked a prosecutor something. Finally, he asked me a few questions about what had happened 10 months ago, and then the final judgement was that I would be "home on 22nd of December".

Boom went his little hammer, and the next person was called in.

It happened so fast that I hadn't even got my head around it yet. I just wasn't ready for it. I had expected a verbal fight, and maybe crying and tears. My brain wasn't working, so I didn't show any sign of happiness at this point. I only nodded and was calmly escorted back to my cell.

And then I got it! All of it!

Only one more month. Only one more month in this shitty, nasty, disgusting prison that had destroyed my health, my mind and even my whole life. Only 33 more nights to endure sleeping on a thin, hard mattress. I would go home, where the quilts are lovely, fresh and clean, and I can sleep whenever I want to!

I will go home!!!

I didn't even care that a policeman would escort me. So what, I would even go in a straitjacket now! I was so excited and happy, just like a little kid!

Dancing around my cell, I turned the TV on louder than usual and jumped up and down with all the rappers on the music channel.

Hurray!

Then my door opened and the guard walked in. She told me off for having the TV on so loud and gave me some paperwork from the trial.

"Can you please translate this for me, madam?"

She nodded and began to read the document out. "Released on 22nd December for good behaviour, half the sentence reduced. Note: release only in the case that all the money is paid to customs for the value of the drugs, which is 200,000 euros."

# 33

# *The Money*

"What?" I said, my stomach burning with pain. "What did you say, madam?"

She read it again.

"You are kidding me now? Are you?"

She shook her head, gave me the paperwork and told me once again to turn the TV down. The door closed again.

I went down on my knees with the papers in my hands, my euphoria gone. I felt like I had fallen down a big, deep, bottomless hole.

*Fuck you, French! What do you see in me? I don't have gold hair, my father is not an oil millionaire and I am not from the Hilton family. How the hell could I have that kind of money? This country doesn't care about the law, only money. Only money! I am not someone with a stash of drugs money back home, stuffed in my old socks for a rainy day.*

I had worked in the prison for a whole year here. Didn't that count? Before that, I'd worked my whole life! Most of the women in prison had never had a job in their whole life or paid tax!

I was really, really pissed off now. It was unbelievable and angry tears flowed.

I was with terrible people in a terrible situation and needed some kind of human contact!

Matilda gave me a hug when I saw her in the shower that evening and cried with me. Her reason for crying probably wasn't that I would not be leaving soon, but she supported me and even lent me her dressing gown.

\* \* \*

Two days later, the psychologist called me.

He had received a letter from prisoners that told him I was having a sexual relationship with Matilda.

I started to laugh. "And this now?" I said, laughing like I'd gone mad. I felt like a mad person too. Who wouldn't go crazy, with all this bullshit around?

The psychologist just stared at me and nervously shifted in his chair.

"Ivana, this is no reason to laugh."

But I kept laughing, and then slowly shifted from laughing to crying. First of all quietly, and then gradually building up to hysterical sobs.

The psychologist just watched and didn't say a word.

"I am so sorry," I told him later. I had no idea how long I had sobbed. I felt like a mad person who had no longer had any idea about time. "Is it getting too much now?"

"Well done, you scored. You got your diploma very successfully," he smiled.

I told him all about the trial and the final judgment, as well as the money, which I didn't have. I told him that my family was not rich and my boyfriend was not in touch.

"Where the hell can I get 197,000 euros from?" I asked in desperation. When I said the price out loud, I started to laugh crazily again and slid back into crying.

"Why can some women go home without paying anything? What I am doing wrong, what's the problem?"

The psychologist sighed, put his hands behind his head and stared out of the window.

"I will try to find some kind of solution. This is really strange."

He waited until I had stopped laughing and crying, and then walked me to the door.

Later on that afternoon, I wrote a letter to the prison and told them I had got absolutely nothing, no money at all. I then sent one letter to a judge, one to Customs, and one to the prison manager.

I couldn't do any more than that for the time being. I had to fight for myself now and use all my energy in this battle.

Matilda was thinking the same, only she saw things differently. That evening, in the showers, she started to fight the Brazilian girl who had talked bullshit about us sleeping together.

I tried to stop her and pull her away, but she leapt at her with her fists. The other women in the showers just stared. They were all used to this kind of show. When they started to shout out, Matilda pushed the Brazilian girl on the hard, tiled floor. She fell down badly and the floor was covered with blood.

"Matilda!" I shouted. "Stop Matilda!"

"Blood, blood, blood. She's killed her!" The rest of them were screaming by now. The water stopped running, the guards came in, and Matilda got herself a few extra months in prison.

She had fought back against the lies, but I didn't understand where all this aggression was coming from. It seemed that this happy bunny, who never took anything seriously, had flipped.

But then again, everyone goes crazy in a different way.

# 34

## *Finally*

The days were really dragging. Winter in Paris was just like a Russian war. I stopped going into the garden and even the library didn't interest me anymore, as I had already read all the books, some of them twice. The closer it got to Christmas, the less work we had.

Just as I was writing one of my long letters to John, I was called for a visit.

"A visit for me?" I asked.

"Yes," my favourite guard answered. "There is some policeman waiting for you."

"Policeman?"

Oh my God, perhaps the cute black guy has come to pick me up. Maybe, when I walk into the room, he will get down on his knees, get out a ring out and ask me to marry him.

I started to laugh and the guard looked at me funnily.

"Sorry, madam, I feel half crazy."

She smiled.

It was a policeman, for sure, but I didn't know him.

"I've got good news for you," he said.

"Yes?"

"I am from the police, I have come to sort out some paperwork. You are going home on Monday."

I just stared at him, unable to say a word. After a minute, I took a breath. "Are you sure? It's not some kind of joke or mistake? Could you please check it again?"

He looked at the paperwork. "You are Ivana Ivancakova, born in Slovakia?"

"Yes."

"So, I am in the right place, and you are too. I have got your tickets for Monday, 14th of December."

"Oh my God."

"Are you OK?"

The psychologist must have helped and pushed the right people, so that they understood that I was not a criminal and I didn't print money at home.

After that, I passed out.

# 35

## Saying Goodbye

My body couldn't take any more of these emotional slaps in the face. First, I was happy, then disappointed, and then euphoric again. It was very tiring now because these intense feelings always became extreme and took up so much energy.

I woke up in a doctor's office, swallowed the pill he gave me and stayed lying down. My eyes were closed, but I could still see everything clearly in my mind's eye. My brain slowly started to digest the information that I was finally going home.

I could see my parents' house. It would be decorated for Christmas and Mum would be baking all the Christmas biscuits and cakes, while Daddy marked down on the TV guide which programmes he wanted to watch over the Christmas period. My brother would be getting off the train with a backpack.

I also saw John getting off the tube, staring at me, and Alisha running across the road, late for work. I don't think I ever felt so light and happy in my whole life, but I didn't have the energy to show it. Apart from a slight smile, you wouldn't have known I was happy because what if everything got messed up? What would happen then?

I said goodbye to Marie and Matilda at the showers, but also wrote letters to them because I could say a lot more in letters than in person. A guard promised she would pass them on after I left.

"I am so happy for you," Matilda said, giving me a hug, with her eyes full of tears. "You don't deserve to be here."

I felt bad that I was leaving them both in prison. It's strange how the difference between guilty and innocent women blurs in prison. It didn't matter how you ended up there, you just try to help each other in whatever way you can.

"I will miss you," Matilda said.

Marie only waved, as it was a very difficult time for her with Christmas, family, children, fights, poison, ambulance, and prison all having happened only last year. These memories had taken over.

I wanted to find a way to tell my parents that I'd be home for Christmas. Not just that, but I would also make it for my birthday! If I wanted to make a call, I had to apply at least two days in advance, but as it was Friday evening with the weekend on the way, that couldn't happen. So my return back home would be a surprise. No one would be waiting for me. Never mind, I would be there, with them. Somehow, I would get there.

\* \* \*

On Monday morning, I packed a few things for Marie and Matilda, even though I had doubts as to whether they would get them. I didn't have a bad relationship with any of the guards, but you never knew what would go missing. After that, I sat down and waited, as I didn't have anything to pack for myself.

This "holiday", however, took much more than it gave me.

# 36

## *Going Home*

Two undercover policemen escorted me to Bratislava. They were supposed to pass me to the Slovak police, who should have escorted me home to my parents in the east of Slovakia.

In the morning, I had to go through all the necessary procedures – my fingerprints, money and luggage. I even had to wear handcuffs once again as I walked through the long halls. I don't even know how many doors I passed.

"Why do I have to wear handcuffs?" I asked a good-looking policewoman that was escorting me, but she didn't answer.

Aha, Miss Important. Well, if that makes her happy...

After the big gates closed behind us, I saw the December sunshine from a different angle, not just from my prison window or the tiny garden.

I took a deep breath.

After one short stop at the police station, when my handcuffs were taken off and I was given a glass of water, I was sitting in a big car with a two young men. My escorts.

We parked in an underground garage and walked through the private security area of the airport. I was smiling now because I didn't feel like a woman who had just left prison. I felt like a celebrity with two bodyguards.

At Prague airport, we had to wait four hours for a plane to Bratislava.

"Would you like to do anything specific or special?" one of the policemen asked me.

I shook my head. "I would like some coffee, sweets and to log onto Facebook. I will not bother you."

And that was what happened. I went to the toilet and put some make-up on. But most of it was a write-off. My mascara had dried out, the foundation had a strange smell, and my bag was a mess.

No problem.

I put on my sunglasses and, via the internet, went back to the real world – the world that I was ripped out of 10 long months ago, and was now returning back to.

Bruised and weak, I was ready to start living my life again.

# *Epilogue*

John called on New Year's Day. My cousin, Danka, had let him know I was out of prison, after I ended up on her doorstep in Bratislava and stayed there for a sleepover.

I picked up the phone back at my parents' home.

"Ivana?"

I started to cry as soon as I heard his voice.

He cried too.

"I am so sorry, so sorry," he said.

I wasn't able to speak, wasn't able to do anything but hold the phone and cry.

Since then, he has called me every day.

I didn't feel like returning to London just yet. I was enjoying being looked after by my mum, sleeping, taking long walks and sleeping again.

Apparently, I was talking in my sleep, and I didn't even move in bed because when you sleep on a thin prison mattress, you wake up every time you turn around.

\* \* \*

When I returned to London, exactly a year after being arrested in Paris, I wanted only one thing – to live a full and calm life.

Today, I live with John in a flat. I cook chicken and try to be a good cook. He does look after me, for most of the time, so I now eat all of my dinner.

And nearly every morning, I get my blueberry muffin.

I don't talk about prison or my doubts, or why he didn't try to contact me.

Apparently, he was dealing with it in his own way. He said that he should have never let me go to Argentina. He couldn't protect me. I was so stroppy back then, I wouldn't listen to anybody or let them tell me what to do!

I don't look back anymore.

I do not care.

I tried so hard to push my name out in the fashion circles, but those people don't remember me anymore, or don't want to. I have stopped trying to be Kate Moss. This year, I didn't even make it to London Fashion Week. I want a baby, to be a good make-up artist or stylist, a job and a calm life with John by my side.

I want to live my life in a way that means I will never, ever have to cry again.

Because big, strong, happy girls don't cry!!!!! ☺

*Keep in touch with me on Instagram @ivkaivus*

# *Thanks To*

A massive thank you to all my friends, the people that know me and my family, for all their support.

Another massive thank you to my cousin, Danka, who is my great support. I would not have been able to make it to where I am now without her. Special thanks to my mum, dad and brother, who did everything they could to help me back to normal life.

Thank you also to my second family, Jane and Adrian W., who are fab. Thank you to Miranda, Elisha and the girls, and Wendy.

Thanks to Matilda, who was my support in that "hell", to Anicka, who was always trying to cheer me up with her long letters, and to my other half; it is not easy to be with me. ☺

A massive thank you to Evita Press, my Slovak publisher, without whom this book would never have happened. Thanks to Leila and I_AM Self-Publishing for their support and the opportunity to work together. Thanks to Adi Alfa and @Bossmedia for your support with this project, and to the lovely Monika Tame (www.monikatame.com), for taking the photo on the cover of this book.